COWLEY PUBLICATIONS is a ministry of the Society of Saint John the Evangelist, a religious community of men in the Episcopal Church. Emerging from the Society's tradition of prayer, theological reflection, and diversity of mission, the press is centered in the rich heritage of the Anglican Communion. Cowley Publications seeks to provide books, audio cassettes, CDs, and other resources for the ongoing theological exploration and spiritual development of the Episcopal Church and others in the body of Christ. To this end, it is dedicated to developing a new generation of theological writers, encouraging them to produce timely, creative, and stimulating publications of excellence, and making these publications available widely, reaching both clergy and lay persons.

*A Matter of
Life and Death:*
Preaching at
Funerals

A Matter of
Life and Death:
Preaching at
Funerals

CHARLES HOFFACKER

Cowley Publications
Cambridge, Massachusetts

Published in the United States of America by Cowley Publications, a division of the Society of Saint John the Evangelist. No portion of this book may be reproduced, stored in or introduced into a retrieval system, or transmitted, in any form or by any means—including photocopying—without the prior written permission of Cowley Publications, except in the case of brief quotations embedded in critical articles and reviews.

Library of Congress Cataloging-in-Publication Data:
Hoffacker, Charles, 1953–
    A matter of life and death : preaching at funerals / Charles Hoffacker.
        p. cm.
Includes bibliographical references.
    ISBN 1-56101-215-7 (alk. paper)
    1. Funeral sermons. 2. Preaching. 3. Church work with the bereaved.
I. Title.
    BV4275.H64 2003
    251'.1—dc21
                                2003001716

Scripture quotations are taken from *The New Revised Standard Version of the Bible*, © 1989, by the Division of Christian Education of the National Council of the Churches of Christ in the United States of America. Used by permission.

Cover art: *Young Buckeye Tree*, 1973: Kathie Bunnell. Stained glass.

This book was printed by Transcontinental Printing in Canada on acid-free paper.

Cowley Publications
907 Massachusetts Avenue
Cambridge, Massachusetts 02139
800-225-1534 • www.cowley.org

Contents

Acknowledgments

Some years back, Robin Harris suggested that my sermons be published. I'm grateful to her for this vote of confidence. My good friend Richard Donovan urged me to contact Cowley Publications; he has given abundant support to this project and to my preaching in general. I'm indebted as well to the congregations of St. Peter's Episcopal Church, Akron, Ohio and St. Paul's Episcopal Church, Port Huron, Michigan for the opportunity to minister among them, especially on occasions which were matters of life and death.

The staff of Cowley Publications have been models of courtesy and thoughtfulness. Susan M. S. Brown deftly edited the manuscript, making this a stronger book than it would have been otherwise.

I'm grateful as always to my wife Cindy Guthrie and our daughter Sophia Hoffacker who are in their own ways ministers of truth and grace.

Charles Hoffacker
Port Huron, Michigan

ONE

Why Preach at a Funeral?

THE PHONE RINGS, AND THE PASTOR ANSWERS. THE voice on the other end announces a death, and asks if the pastor will take the funeral. Suddenly the pastor knows that the shape of the next several days will be very different from what he or she had been expecting only moments before. Certain activities must now be canceled, postponed, or squeezed in somehow. There will be people to contact at church, a meeting to attend at the funeral home, a liturgy to plan, a sermon to write, an appearance at the visitation, church preparations, the service, the luncheon, the burial.

Many people will be involved in the events of the next several days: funeral home staff; the family, friends, and neighbors of the deceased; the church's organist, altar guild, and sexton; the people responsible for the bereavement meal; the employees at the cemetery or crematorium. Each person will play an important part, for only close teamwork can bring off these events. The pastor's role will be manifold: grief counselor, liturgy designer, officiant, community chaplain, coordinator of church personnel and resources.

But one aspect of the pastor's role will be more public, more verbal, than anything else done during this process. It is the responsibility of "saying something" at the funeral. These words will not be like the personal reminiscences of friends and family, those funny, poignant, meaningful recollections sometimes punctuated by sobs or laughter. Not only will the pastor recite the words of scripture and liturgy, important as those are, but he or she will also offer more personal words as a preacher, the one designated to speak of eternal life in the face of this particular, painfully real death. These words must somehow be God's own good news, though one of God's dear children lies dead.

The words preached by the pastor constitute a work of translation. Liturgy and hymnody, scripture and sacrament are made accessible and immediate through the message from the pulpit. They are not necessarily incomprehensible without the sermon, but the sermon can make them strangely fresh and new. Yet for many contemporary listeners, the language of traditional Christianity is well nigh incomprehensible, so it becomes all the more important that the preacher render the Christian story into a version that can touch their hearts. Efforts to do this will not go unrewarded.

The preacher speaks today's language, yet with a Christian accent. He or she thus stands out in a society whose public behavior is overwhelmingly secular. The preacher also stands out because of the freedom with which he or she speaks about death and violence and hope. The preacher presents death not as an irksome problem or an embarrassment, but as the dark door leading to the fulfillment of a welcome promise. Our society is largely numb to violence, but the pastor does not hesitate to name it as an obscenity. Our secular society can find little to say about the higher hopes of humanity, but the preacher incarnates these hopes in speech and thus contributes to their fulfillment.

The role of funeral preacher challenges and stretches the pastor no matter how many funerals he or she has taken before. The pastor knows that the expectations are high. People gathered for the funeral will have real needs—for consolation, for hope, for making sense of what seems senseless—and they look to the pastor for the means to meet these needs. Anyone who preaches knows the weakness of human language, how easily it splits apart when made into a container for the holy. Preachers know the weakness of their own language, how sometimes, despite the best efforts, communication does not occur. So wise preachers will pray to be overshadowed by the Spirit, as was Mary, the mother of the Lord, in the hope that Christ will be born alive again in the country of death.

Some in the congregation that day will be people of deep spirituality, deeper perhaps than the preacher's own. Others will be thoroughly secular people, perhaps scornful of religion, uncomfortable inside a church, and wanting only to honor the dead and comfort the living; yet at this moment, up against the nagging puzzle of human mortality, they will be uniquely open to the

Gospel's intrusion into their lives. Many of those present will claim a Christian identity, and even membership in a church, with some degree of hesitation, and will want their faith to provide solace in the face of death. Whatever their reasons for coming, the crowd who assembles for a funeral are often more ready to listen to the preacher than is the usual Sunday congregation, because what brings people together at the funeral is undeniably a matter of life and death.

↶ The Ambiguity of Death

The deceased may be a perfect stranger to the pastor or a dear friend, a faithful parishioner or someone on the margins of congregational life. The death may have struck as suddenly as a car crash or heart attack. It may have come as a welcome conclusion after months, even years, of lingering illness. Those gathered may mourn the loss of a baby, a child, a teenager, a young adult, someone in middle age, or someone alive for most of a century. Every funeral is different, because every life is different, uniquely precious.

Each type of funeral brings its challenges. When the deceased is a perfect stranger, taking her or his funeral can feel like walking into a theater just as the play is over and wondering what happened before. The occasion can seem like parachuting into the midst of that person's family and friends, who may themselves be unsure how to respond to this unknown presence in their midst.

With a dear friend, the pastor is likely to lose objectivity, feel out of focus, and store up his or her own grief for some later time. On rare, graced occasions, however, the pastor may somehow manage to be both heavy-hearted mourner and effective preacher, the one who heals whose own wound is obvious.

In the case of the faithful parishioner, the pastor senses the loss of a companion, a table mate at the Supper of the Lord. A faint voice of guilt may sound in the pastor's mind: How could I have ministered more effectively to this person during our years together, and at the end? But a quiet word of mercy may also speak: Here is a good and faithful servant of the Lord; helping people to become such, supporting them, is part of what the pastor's vocation is all about.

When the deceased lived at the margins of parish life, there can also be interior questions about the effectiveness of the parish's and the pastor's ministry. Never underestimate the ability of the conscientious mind to torment itself! Dealing with the survivors can feel awkward. The interactions may highlight unasked questions about whether the deceased felt a part of this Christian community, and whether the survivors feel that they belong.

Yet each of these circumstances, also bestows a distinct opportunity. To bury the stranger has a wonderful clearness. It is a work of mercy, an outreach to both the dead and the living. The pastor is invited into the circle of family and friends, trusted at a time of their greatest vulnerability. The stranger's funeral bears witness to the bonds that unite all people and that our common humanity has been assumed and redeemed by Christ.

To bury a friend is both a privilege and an opportunity

to render service, and is likely to appear more often as the pastor ages, particularly if he or she exercises a long pastorate in the same place. The question "What can I do?" receives a concrete, realistic answer: "Be pastor and preacher for the funeral of your friend." The preacher then bears effective witness to how grace was at work in that particular life. This witness is marked by discretion, gratitude, and authenticity, all of them fruits of a friendship that has entered a new stage.

When the funeral is for a parishioner, an active one or someone at the margins of the congregation, the pastor engages in one of the primary functions of the pastorate. An opportunity arises to enter more deeply into the power of the Gospel than may be possible during other parish activities. The funeral knits the congregation together through the sharing of sorrow and hope. This specific reminder of life's shortness and uncertainty awakens pastor and people to what really matters, what abides beyond all else.

Where death strikes quickly, the mourners may well be in shock, and the grieving have barely begun. Following a lengthy illness, some of the grieving may already be past. Yet even when death is not a surprise, still it brings fresh grief. A lingering death may mean that the grief is mingled with an awkward sense of relief, first that the loved one is no longer in pain, and also that the survivors' lives can begin to return to normal. These feelings connected with death, strongest in those closest to the deceased, have echoes in the pastor as well.

Death beyond a certain age usually suggests completeness. The feeling of tragedy is muted. The funeral may well convey the sense of a life well-lived, of decades put to good use. Death before a certain age, however, incites agony over a life that looks incomplete, unlived, with the loss of untold opportunities. Death's cruelty then seems especially bitter. Questions of meaning come to the surface. The pastor's homiletical task is far harder when the body in the casket still bears the beauty of youth, or even the innocence of childhood.

∽ From Creation to Consummation

The church year repeats itself. What the preacher doesn't talk about this Christmas can be covered next Christmas. But somebody's death and burial indicates that Christianity is characterized less by cycles than by a linear sense of time. Linear time moves from creation to consummation. This is true of both the entire cosmos and a single human life. When somebody dies, whether after a few hours or ten decades, there is only that moment in which to speak the Gospel to the sharp, fresh pain of the survivors. It is necessary to write a word of hope in the concrete of their experience before it hardens.

Stubbornness or strong coffee may be necessary to keep the pastor alert in the early morning hours, crafting a homily for a funeral soon to happen. Yet a little extra effort is not too much to demand on such an occasion. In one sense, the deceased lived a lifetime preparing the way for this word of grace. If liturgy can be compared to theater, then a funeral is a play that opens and closes the same night. There is only this one chance to do it well.

Perhaps for the pastor it will be the third funeral in as many weeks or as many days. The stream of homiletical wisdom may be reduced to a trickle. Perhaps the pastor is afflicted by personal issues and distractions, large or small. Perhaps she or he has had to set on the shelf too much personal grief, vowing to deal with it when there is time. Still, something must be said at this funeral too. Weak though the message may appear to the pastor, to the congregation it must sound and look and smell of the early hours of Easter morning, and thus beckon them out of this latest Good Friday darkness.

Preparing to preach at a funeral kindles the remembrance of other deaths, other encounters with grief, other funerals. The pastor cannot forget that sometimes he or she has been among the mourners out in the pews. Preparing to preach at a funeral reminds the pastor that somewhere down the road death awaits, even for him or her. Sermons generally need to be directed to the homilist as well as to others. Similarly, every funeral sermon must have something to say to the preacher about his or her own death.

∿ An Unparalleled Opportunity

Do all funerals have sermons? For Anglicans, rubrics can answer this question one way, but a theology of proclamation requires a different answer.

The three burial services in *The Book of Common Prayer* of the Episcopal Church permit a homily but do not require it. The Burial of the Dead: Rite One declares in a rubric after the reading of the Gospel, "A homily may be preached, the people being seated." Fortunately, the people's right to sit down at this time is stated explicitly! But who will deliver this homily and whether there will even be one remain open questions. The corresponding rubric in the Burial of the Dead: Rite Two states: "Here there may be a homily by the Celebrant, or a member of the family, or a friend." Strictly understood, this rubric would disallow a homily by another member of the clergy, unless that cleric were "a member of the family, or a friend"! However, there is wisdom in allowing homilists other than the clergy on this occasion. The outline entitled An Order for Burial states simply that "a homily may follow the Readings." Again, the question of the homilist is left open.

While *The Book of Common Prayer* usually speaks of sermons, these directions refer to a homily, perhaps suggesting that the speaker need not meet the requirements of canon law concerning preachers. Of greater significance is the fact that, in every case, a homily is permitted but not required.

The Book of Alternative Services of the Anglican Church of Canada takes a slightly different approach. A rubric in the Form I Funeral Liturgy for Use in Church states, "The celebrant welcomes the congregation and may at this time, or after the readings, express thanksgiving for the gifts of the deceased person, especially the marks of a Christian life. Such remarks, without denying the legitimate grief of the mourners, should relate the life and death of the Christian to the victory of Christ." These "remarks" would seem to constitute a funeral homily or sermon, however short or informal.

The Form II Funeral Liturgy repeats this rubric, and adds another between those concerned with the readings and the Apostles' Creed: "A brief sermon may be preached if the celebrant's greeting of the congregation has not been extensive." What is meant by a brief sermon or a not-extensive greeting is not explained; such is the restraint characteristic of Anglican rubrics. Nor does the Form identify who will preach the sermon.

In every case, the sermon or remarks are optional; In this matter, *The Book of Alternative Services* and *The Book of Common Prayer* unite in stating that preaching is not required at funerals. However, my conviction is that, whatever latitude the rubrics provide, in the liturgy few if any funerals will not be enriched by an effective sermon or homily. I believe that those responsible for funerals should treat the homily or sermon as a normal, integral part of the service.

A sermon is a response to God's Word proclaimed in the scripture readings, especially the Gospel. The liturgical response to this proclamation often includes elements in addition to the sermon, such as a creed, intercessions, and a confession of sin. Indeed, all that happens in the liturgy subsequent to the readings can be understood as a response to the Word that has been proclaimed. This holds true for both Eucharistic and non-Eucharistic services.

Even if unusual instances should call for no sermon in the usual sense of a spoken address, the service would likely be enriched by some response to the Word of God in scripture. Only a response of this sort could address the congregation and confront the immediate situation with directness.

The Order for Celebrating the Holy Eucharist in *The Book of Common Prayer* indirectly addresses how such a response to the Word can be made in a funeral service. This outline of elements essential to a Eucharistic liturgy includes the following:

⌣ Proclaim and Respond to the Word of God

The proclamation and response may include readings, song, talk, dance, instrumental music, other art forms, silence. A reading from the Gospel is always included.

Here the list of forms that proclamation and response can take is suggestive, not exhaustive. A given activity may be proclamation, response, or both. God's Word can be proclaimed and opportunity be provided to respond to that Word even before a creed or the Prayers of the People. This is an appropriate principle for funerals, including ones where the Eucharist is not celebrated.

Not only is God's Word proclaimed at a funeral through scripture, but there must be response to that Word, often through several activities. Among the circle of family and friends there may be people whose skills and experience eminently qualify them to respond to the Word through a number of art forms. Response may even engage any members of the congregation who wish to participate, so long as the activity does not demand too much. For example, the pastor might provide the mourners with an opportunity to write down reasons they are grateful for the life of the deceased. These reasons can then be collected and offered at the altar.

As noted, this book takes the perspective that a sermon is a normal part of the funeral service, even if not an absolutely necessary one. If a sermon is not included, there still must be adequate opportunity for a response to the Word proclaimed through scripture. I regard the sermon as normative because a funeral offers such a significant moment for pastoral ministry, a chance to offer the Gospel at a time of crisis. Death, that mystery from which none of us is exempt, demands an answer from Christian faith, one that is not simply generic but tailored to the realities of each situation. Preaching is an important way to communicate this answer.

It is hard for me to understand a regular lack of preaching at funerals as anything other than the loss of unparalleled opportunities to present the Gospel of Christ to both believers and nonbelievers. Some people present at a funeral are experiencing deep anguish over the loss of someone close to them. All of those present deserve to hear the message of Christ's victory over death in a way that is immediate and effective.

⌁ Spreading Rumors of Resurrection

If what people tell me of their experiences with funerals is a fair sampling, then many are eager to hear through the funeral sermon a word of hope, a rumor of resurrection. Too often this expectation is not met. Far too many funeral homilies come across to far too many listeners as uncaring, impersonal, trivial, or just plain ineffective. These failings may result in part from inadequate preaching skills or incomplete preparation, but they may also reflect a fundamental misconception of the aim of a funeral homily or the lack of an effective method for achieving that aim.

Christian preaching has been described as holding the Bible in one hand and the daily newspaper in the other. If so, then funeral sermons involve holding the Bible in one hand and a clipped obituary notice in the other. Both Bible and obituary are necessary. But frequently the funeral sermon involves only the obituary notice or only the Bible.

Sometimes what passes for preaching at a funeral is in fact a eulogy. What I mean by eulogy is an address that celebrates the high character and significant achievements of the deceased. Eulogies have their place, perhaps even in church, but a eulogy is *not* a funeral sermon. Eulogies are not primarily concerned with Christ's victory over death or the participation of the deceased in that victory. Eulogies look backward to a completed earthly life, not forward to the consummation of that life with God. They consider human character, not the divine grace that shapes that character. The eulogy is what happens when one hand raises the obituary notice and the other hand does not raise the Bible.

Even if eulogies could serve as funeral sermons, there are many funerals where a eulogy would be inappropriate. Everyone the Church buries is a sinner, but people who persist in notorious sin, or whose character and achievements give no cause for celebration, are clearly not fit candidates for eulogizing.

Another unsatisfactory alternative to the funeral sermon involves raising up the Bible but not the obituary notice. What results is a generalized religious message that takes no account of the deceased or the needs of the mourners. This is the "canned" homily, full of heavenly references perhaps, but of absolutely no earthly good.

The nightmare extreme of this alternative is the message that does not mention the dead person by name or refer to her or his life or circumstances. Thus a stranger entering the church, knowing nothing about the deceased, might be unable to infer from the message even the deceased's sex and age. People in the pews resent such abstract platitudes, and their resentment is justified.

There is a body in a casket, ashes in an urn, or at least tearful mourners only a few feet from the pulpit, yet these tangible, visible realities are overlooked. In an attempt to address all deaths, the generalized religious message fails to address the one right at hand.

The need to lift up both the Bible and the obituary notice bears witness to a basic principle in Christianity: holding polarities in a dynamic relationship. Theology and practice include an important series of "both ... and" realities. God is both three and one. Christ is both human and divine. Creation is both contingent and real. The Christian is both a sinner and justified. The list goes on, and is so inclusive of what is central to Christianity that anything without this rhythm of "both ... and" may be justly regarded as inadequate, suspect, or even heretical.

The funeral sermon must be a "both ... and" reality. The obituary notice must be lifted up; so too must the

Bible, and they must be lifted together. The connection between the two must be discovered, asserted, insisted upon. What the preacher does, in front of pews filled with mourners, is a daring act. He or she relates the life and death of this particular deceased person and the grief of these particular mourners to the universal hope manifest in Christ's suffering and triumph. Thus the obituary notice finds its proper place with the pages of the Bible.

To make this connection, however lamely, between a particular human death and the universal hope available in Christ is to succeed at funeral preaching. To fall short of this connection, or even fail to attempt it, is grounds for a charge of homiletical malpractice. Within the circle of mourners, what must be proclaimed is the resurrection, though it seems foolish under the circumstances. The preacher needs to remember the origins of Christian proclamation: how early one morning women went to complete funeral arrangements that had been postponed. In that context they encountered something, someone, they had not expected. And so the funeral arrangements were forever thwarted. Those women fled the tomb with what was the first Christian funeral sermon, which became the basis for all others.

Two

Finding the Key

USUALLY THE PERIOD BETWEEN A DEATH AND FUNERAL is only a few days. It is a liminal time for the survivors, when they are confronted starkly with issues of life and death. It is also a demanding time for the preacher, who must prepare for the funeral and the events around it and face the same issues from her or his own perspective. Time has ended for the deceased, but it does not stand still for the survivors. Instead, death's reality and its urgent demands, particularly in the short term, are overlaid onto the ordinary flow of time and activities.

Effective funeral preaching requires using this brief period to its best advantage. Amid a flurry of arrangements and activities, the pastor needs to assume a contemplative stance and listen in a disciplined way. The preacher waits for what I will call the key to the funeral sermon. This key helps mourners recognize grace in the unique life of the deceased. It helps the preacher proclaim good news in the face of this particular death.

The key may be an image, a phrase, a story, a personal characteristic, a vocation or avocation, or some other feature that is connected with, or at least *can* be connected with the life of the deceased. It is the obvious centerpiece of the sermon. Beyond that, however, this key unlocks something in the memories of the mourners. It brings the life of the deceased to their awareness in a new way, one that serves the proclamation of the Gospel. It helps them consider the deceased not only in terms of death and loss, but also in the unconquerable light of Christ's resurrection.

The key may be a biographical detail, however large or small, that connects with the mourners' entire memory of the deceased. This memory has been traumatized by the death, and the mourners await a word of hope, a rumor of resurrection. Through the key, the Gospel message enters into the mourners, not in a generalized way but in one that addresses their unique grief. In the preacher's words the mourners recognize that God's Spirit is at large in the world, and that this Spirit is stronger than death. They realize how God was at work in the life of the deceased. They come to accept that, though the deceased is now dead to the world, he or she is not dead to God. The key enables the mourners to discover grace and resurrection anew (or for the first time), specifically in the circumstances around this death. The mourners experience an "aha!" moment of revelation, inspired by Christian hope.

The key gets the preacher around the difficulty frequently experienced in preaching at the funeral of someone she or he did not know or barely knew. In a legitimate way, the preacher "takes advantage" of the mourners' extensive knowledge of the one who has died. The preacher invites them to examine anew the life of the deceased in the expectation that they will see how "to your faithful people, O Lord, life is changed, not ended."

◟ Unlocking a Mystery

Finding the key demands expectant listening by the preacher. Thus the preacher does well to spend time with the survivors whenever possible, within the limits of practicality and pastoral sensitivity. Opportunities can include the time right around the death, whether at home, in a hospital, or elsewhere; the planning session at the funeral home; and visiting hours leading up to the funeral. Sometimes the pastor will be present around the time of death or will be called in when death is imminent or has just occurred. Pastors should make it a habit of attending funeral planning sessions. They should instruct parishioners that, as *The Book of Common Prayer* states, "The death of a member of the Church should be reported as soon as possible to, and arrangements for the funeral should be made in consultation with, the Minister of the Congregation." Parishioners should be reminded of this instruction in a pastorally appropriate way when a death is likely to occur soon. Responsible funeral directors will appreciate the participation of the clergy in the discussion of arrangements, and may even come to avoid funeral planning without the pastor present.

Pastors should also make a standard practice of attending visiting hours, whether these are held at a funeral home or at the church. Sometimes an opportunity for prayer with the mourners will emerge; at other times, the visitation should best be let run its course. In any case, the appearance of the pastor, if only for a brief period, makes an important statement about the church's concern for both the living and the dead.

There are good pastoral reasons for the clergy to be present at these three times—at the planning of the funeral, at the visitation, and at the funeral itself— but such events also provide invaluable opportunities to discover a key to effective proclamation at the funeral. The people present will speak about the deceased and how he or she was significant to them. In offhand, even humorous remarks, they may reveal something of the character of the one they have come to mourn. The pastor is likely to gain new and significant information about the deceased, even if their acquaintance goes back for decades.

Sometimes conversation during calling hours will focus on the final illness, the accident, or other fresh events. At other times the focus will be on the past. It may be appropriate for the pastor to ask people for their memories of the deceased, especially if there is an awkward (rather than helpful) silence. The increasingly common practice of video or photo displays at visitations can sometimes provide a visual key for preaching or at least a starting point for conversation with mourners.

The pastor should be open to details in the home, the hospital, and even the community in which the deceased lived. The pastor should also be attentive to details in his or her own life during the days leading up to the funeral. Sometimes these may provide a key for presenting this particular death in the light of God's grace.

The scheduling of a memorial service or a funeral with ashes present can respond more to the convenience of the family than can a funeral with a body and casket, which may result in a longer period between death and the liturgy. In such cases, the preacher has additional time in which to discern the key and develop the sermon. Occasionally, when the pastor has been acquainted with an older parishioner over a period of years, she or he may become aware before the parishioner dies of the key for that person's funeral sermon.

Whatever the time period between a death and the liturgy, the pastor's recognition of this key can itself be an experience of grace. Like the insights behind other sermons, this key may erupt into conscious awareness at an unexpected time, for example, when the would-be preacher is taking a shower or driving along a familiar road. Its appearance can be awaited with expectancy but can never be forced. The preacher must prepare to recognize and receive the gift and to make the best use of it.

Discovering the key is an experience of God's kingdom like that of the woman who loses a silver coin, lights a lamp, and sweeps diligently until she finds it. Once the precious coin is in her hands again, she calls together her friends and neighbors, and invites them to rejoice with her (Luke 15:8–9). As the woman in this parable must share her joy with others, so must the preacher who finds in the midst of death's darkness a key that unlocks grace in the life of the deceased and in the lives of us all.

Thus a focus on the key lifts the preaching challenge above the unacceptable alternatives of a secular eulogy and an abstract religious discourse. It employs the resources of human relationship and insistent grace as they have already been experienced, consciously or not, by the hearers. Yet this key does more than unlock the past at a time of deep loss and pain. It also unlocks the mourners' hearts to receive the gifts of grace, healing, and hope. It calls the mourners to look differently upon this death and all other deaths, including their own. The key can reveal, even in funereal light, a glimmer of light that suggests resurrection.

⌁ A Full Ring of Keys

Every such key is unique, just as each human life has a stubborn uniqueness. The key will often show up unexpectedly, or at least well up from within the depths of the preacher instead of appearing plainly within the life of the deceased. Still it is possible to point to categories of keys. This typology is presented with caution, however, for no doubt other keys also wait to make themselves apparent. Through the abundant grace of God, these categories and keys will become available at a moment between somebody's last breath and when the preacher steps up to the pulpit.

A key may be some feature of our common humanity. Such keys are especially helpful when the preacher is not well acquainted with the deceased. However, care must be taken to avoid an abstract sermon, one not grounded in the life of the deceased as a unique person.

The preacher's task is to establish a significant connection between the person who died and those listening.

A key can also be a characteristic specific to the deceased. Here a behavior, a mannerism, or an expression would be an obvious candidate. This characteristic must be easy to recognize as belonging to the individual, and must also be worth remembering and celebrating. It may be small, but it cannot be trivial. Within the sermon, the characteristic must act not as a trigger to sentimentality but as a witness to grace at work in a human life.

A person's vocation or avocation may also provide the key announcing grace at work in his or her life, while promising glory with God. To highlight such a key, the preacher offers brief reminders of what occupied the deceased over the years and presents this work as contributing to the common good. The preacher should take care, however, to avoid completely identifying someone with his or her occupation.

Some lives present a special challenge for the preacher, for example, those whose full-time "employment" is coping with their serious chronic illness, or others who wreck their lives through addiction, crime, or other destructive paths. In such instances, the sermon may need to recognize the difficulty of locating grace at work in such a sad story. Then the preacher may draft the congregation as the search party! The preacher may call upon them to explore their memories and find where, despite everything, God's fingerprints were on the life of that troubled person. Authentic reasons for gratitude can emerge from these explorations. Such a tribute respects the life of the deceased in its uniqueness and presents it as redeemed by Christ along with all others.

Other lives may be hard to talk about simply because of their strongly private, or perhaps domestic, character. In such cases, the intimacy of the home offers a key for identifying God's grace at work. Care must be taken not to suffocate the congregation with an unreal portrayal of family bliss. A few concrete reminders of a generally happy home life can be enough to call up gratitude as a companion to grief.

As I have said, Christ and the specific Christian are authentic polarities in funeral sermons. Therefore, a consideration of the deceased as a mirror of Christ can be a sermon key. Specifically, if every Christian mirrors Christ, however dimly or imperfectly, then this reality can be put to use in proclaiming the Gospel in the face of each person's death. The deceased can be presented as a mirror of Christ. The preacher need not shout to do this, whether literally or figuratively, but can speak in a manner that is bold and forthright.

Then too, the funeral sermon may present the deceased as someone responding to God, whose relationship with the Lord provides an example for others. Here room must be left for those in the congregation to respond to God in ways appropriate to who they are. They can take hints from the life now over, they can find inspiration in the fidelity demonstrated by the deceased, but their own response must be original, as original as that made by the deceased.

The response to God offered by the deceased may reveal a resemblance between that person and a saint of scripture or church history. The saint's story and example then help to illuminate how grace worked in the life of the deceased. The connection between the newly departed and the celebrated saint suggests that our lives can be additional links in the same holy chain.

The last type of key points us beyond both present and past to ongoing worlds. Sometimes these worlds will be here on earth, as mourners survive their grief and recognize themselves as the living legacy of the departed. The congregation will welcome the suggestion that tomorrow will be better than today.

At other times, the ongoing world will be that place where resurrection power has achieved its purpose. The heaven at which such sermons hint is characterized by a new and wondrous life beyond our best experiences. This life will not consist of mere private satisfaction but be a city centered on the vision of God and the lamb, a corporate life of unending joy and praise, the new Jerusalem to which John points in his Apocalypse. The preacher has the great privilege of presenting this heaven which offers hope on earth, which shines and beckons, and which, by doing so, makes us strong for the journey home.

⌣ The Key to Grace

Again, the key unlocks the history of the deceased to reveal grace at work there. That history is known, to one degree or another, by the mourners. The preacher offers the key, but the listeners put it to use. They use it to open their memories and find God at work in the past of the deceased. (If the deceased was very young, then they open what they expected would be memories.) The listeners simultaneously open their wounded hearts in the hope of finding, through divine action, a healing balm available to them now. They come to trust that the God who worked in the past and works in the present will not cease working in the future, both for themselves and for those they love but see no longer.

An effective sermon will allow mourners to partake of the victory of Jesus Christ over death. Writing the sermon is itself an act of faith, however, for in doing so the pastor acts on the belief that grace is active in every human life, however covertly, and that God will provide an appropriate key for every funeral sermon, a balm for every Gilead of loss and bereavement.

THREE

Constructing the Sermon

IN DISCOVERING THE KEY FOR THE FUNERAL SERMON, the preacher is attentive to such factors as the life and circumstances of the deceased, the facts of that person's death, and the preacher's own experiences around the time of the death. Once the preacher becomes aware of the sermon key, attention shifts to other factors that must be taken into account when constructing the sermon. These include the congregation that will gather for the service, the scripture readings that will be proclaimed, sermon references to the deceased and his or her eternal destiny, the sermon's length, generic ingredients in funeral preaching, and the issue of additional speakers. Above all, the key must be put to its proper use if it is to suggest the gracious, saving activity of God. This requires a contemplative perspective, an intentional listening to life which is intentional.

⌣ The Congregation

This congregation for a funeral will usually be more diverse than the one that gathers on a typical Sunday. It may include people of non-Christian faiths and of no faith, as well as Christians from diverse traditions. Parishioners may well find themselves outnumbered by visitors. Many stages of faith development will be present. There may be people in the pews with serious conflicts about religion in general and Christianity in particular. Some of those present may not have found past funerals helpful, and they may be attending only out of a sense of duty or a desire to "pay respects" to the deceased.

Yet for all its diversity, a funeral congregation also shares a sense of unity which may only rarely be matched on Sunday morning: The people present for a funeral are united by a common grief. To one degree or another, they are all caught up in the same crisis. However religious or nonreligious they may deem themselves, all those present are confronted by issues of grief, loss, and their own mortality. Each may welcome some word of relief, encouragement, or hope. Often the funeral congregation listens with an attention not to be found at an ordinary Sunday service. Perhaps more than at any other time, at a funeral faith proves itself either useful or useless.

Contemporary preachers, especially those in liturgical churches, must realize that many people attending a funeral find themselves in a setting full of unfamiliar images, actions, vocabulary, and meaning. Ritual patterns and the language of faith, so significant to the committed

Christian, constitute unknown territory for many of our neighbors today. This lack of familiarity with Christian basics represents a challenge for preachers, but also an opportunity. These neighbors may be especially susceptible to hearing the Gospel when it is delivered in response to somebody's death. In any event, the preacher does well to see his or her role in conducting a funeral as that of missionary as well as pastor.

✓ Scripture

On a Sunday morning, every member of a congregation is rarely preoccupied by the same recent event. Therefore, the reading of the scriptures becomes an outstanding focus for the congregation as a whole. The sermon may appropriately engage one or more texts in detail in order to apply them to our diverse and complicated world. But scripture plays a different role in the funeral service.

Beyond those passages chosen from scripture, the funeral preacher has another holy text to deal with: the now completed life of a particular Christian. Because this text is complete, it may pressure the preacher more than do the circumstances of those who come to be baptized, confirmed, married, or ordained. There is greater urgency to say something now that a life is over. The mourners need to consider that life, and that death, in the light of Christ's resurrection, to recognize that the deceased shares in Christ's victory over death. All of us, Christian and nonchristian alike, are well acquainted with the power of death in this world. It is imperative that the preacher declare the one power that is stronger than death and link that power with the death that the congregation has assembled to grieve.

Everybody present will claim some awareness of the holy text which is the life of the deceased. What the preacher must do is connect that life text to the unique and powerful hope underlying the scripture texts and the canon to which they belong. Thus, the preacher may subject the readings at a funeral to benign neglect in the sermon, but only if the hope they express is effectively communicated through other means. The language of the liturgy is one such channel of expression. Certainly the funeral services of the Episcopal Church and the Anglican Church of Canada have proven their worth in this regard. Another important channel is carefully chosen hymnody and other music. In this kind of carefully crafted service, the biblical readings are experienced in a rich context that interprets and reinforces their content. For this reason, the scripture passages for a funeral ought to be chosen not arbitrarily but with regard to the character of the deceased and the circumstances of the service.

Placing scripture in the background must not, however, create a vacuum that allows unscriptural or unhelpful notions about life and death to enter. This problem threatens especially when the service takes place in a funeral home. Most funeral home staff deserve high praise for the help they give to grieving people. Yet, by omission or commission, the ethos and practices of such establishments do not necessarily express what the Church attempts to communicate through its preaching and liturgy, music and architecture.

The pastor should never indulge in a muted denial of death, no matter how tasteful, or resort to the liturgical or homiletical equivalent of the pastel colors popular in funeral home leaflets. The Church knows a Lord who died a gruesome death and was raised to life in glory, and it announces this Lord in bold colors: blood flowing from his wounds, the darkness of the tomb, the brilliance of his resurrected face. The funeral home milieu treats death as an unavoidable indignity. St. Paul, however, names death as the last enemy to be destroyed. Christianity has its origin not in a decent burial but in an abandoned grave.

At the end of the burial rites in *The Book of Common Prayer*, a note appears that epitomizes these services. It begins: "The liturgy for the dead is an Easter liturgy. It finds all its meaning in the resurrection. Because Jesus was raised from the dead, we, too, shall be raised." Like the liturgy for the dead, preaching at funerals finds all its meaning in the resurrection of Jesus. It is Easter preaching. A funeral sermon need not be heavy with explicit biblical references, but it must convey the central message of scripture: that nothing, not even death, shall separate us from God's love revealed in Jesus Christ our Lord.

∿ References to the Deceased

Personal references to the deceased connect the Gospel to the immediate situation of death, loss, and grieving. Often the sermon's key will be something personal about the deceased. But just as such references need to be included, they also need to be used with restraint. Brief references will activate the memories of the deceased in ways that extensive narration could never do. The preacher must hold firmly to the belief that the listener brings something to the hearing, a treasure of memory and affection based on relationship with the deceased.

The preacher should be sparing in the use of personal references for another reason as well: The more such references the preacher includes, the more likely that some of them may be inaccurate, perhaps terribly so. The temptation to turn a human being into an inhuman exemplar of goodness is especially strong. When someone dies, we often exalt the person's strengths and overlook weaknesses, and even vices. Within limits this tendency is acceptable. Yet how easily it can get out of hand, aided and abetted through pulpit platitudes. Certainly the preacher ought to celebrate grace at work in the person's life, but he or she should not change the deceased into a plaster saint. It is salutary that the Commendation for Burial Rite Two in *The Book of Common Prayer* speaks of the deceased not only as "a sheep of your own fold, a lamb of your own flock" but also as "a sinner of your own redeeming."

ᐯ The Life to Come

Similar challenges arise when the preacher addresses the eternal destiny of the deceased or the general conditions of the life to come. Here the balance and restraint of Anglican liturgical language offers us trustworthy guidance. At various points in the funeral service as well as elsewhere in public worship, we pray for the departed. The reason we do this is succinctly stated in the Episcopal Catechism: "We pray for them, because we still hold them in our love, and because we trust that in God's presence those who have chosen to serve him will grow in his love, until they see him as he is." In other words, we are still connected by love with those who have died. We trust that the ones for whom we pray are among those who have chosen to serve God. We believe that all such will continue to grow in God's love, at least until they achieve the definitive vision of God.

Yet Anglican services make no guarantees regarding particular persons, and they offer no warrant for preachers to do so. The departed are commended to God's mercy, which is abundantly manifest to us in Christ. On this basis, the sermon may place a departed person with God in the company of the redeemed, but not with the voice of declaration. Instead, the voice must be that of hope, a reasonable, religious, and holy hope, one based on the resurrection of Jesus. This is a hope that the preacher is right to announce and proclaim.

Moreover, the sermon must present salvation always as a matter of grace, of divine mercy, not as something we earn or as something that occurs naturally. What saves us, now and hereafter, what makes sense of our lives at this moment and when our lives are over, is the miracle of God's mercy. The need of some for that mercy may appear to us more obvious than the need of others, but for all of us that need is in reality absolute.

It is important to avoid and counteract any tendency toward a false view of the afterlife. This view can take several forms. One, obviously, is a materialism that denies any life to come. Another, perhaps more insidious, is a sentimentalism that suffocates wonder by depicting a heaven unworthy of either God or humanity, a salvation that comes not by free but by cheap grace.

Related to this perspective is the view which the New Testament associates with the Sadducees. They denied the resurrection because they could not imagine an afterlife different from this world and dismissed an afterlife identical to this world as nonsensical. In support of their view, they proposed the case of the woman who had married and buried a series of brothers, and asked whose wife she would be in the resurrection (Matthew 22:23–33; Mark 12:18–27; Luke 20:27–40). There are those today who believe in an afterlife but cannot imagine it to be different from life on earth. They believe in survival rather than resurrection, a mere continuation of life rather than a new life. One version of this belief is to imagine that, for the avid golfer on earth, the next life contains no higher joy than uninterrupted golf in heaven.

The challenge in every case is to assert an afterlife, one connected with life here on earth yet wondrously exceeding our earthly categories and experiences. As in Jesus' parables about the kingdom, the funeral sermon must deal with heaven by suggesting it rather than describing it. While presenting heaven as an object of hope and expectation, the preacher's approach to it must also be characterized by wonder and surprise.

✒ Sermon Length and Generic Ingredients

How long should the funeral sermon be? Only long enough to say what needs to be said! The length will vary considerably. It has been wisely observed that the length and structure of a sermon often mimic the length and structure of the scriptural passage on which it is based. There may be a similar correspondence between the funeral sermon and the key upon which it is based.

In addition, the preacher may include certain standard ingredients into many of her or his funeral sermons. For instance, a review of the purposes for the gathering may orient members of the congregation. A sermon could refer to gathering in mutual support, hearing the Good News, giving thanks for the life of the deceased, and praying for that person and ourselves. A congregation may need to be reminded that grief is legitimate and that sorrow bears witness to our love. The preacher can also encourage those gathered for the funeral to share their stories of the deceased, not only on that day but in the future, and not only among the contemporaries of the deceased but among his or her descendants.

✒ Additional Speakers

Questions may arise regarding additional speakers, family members or friends who want to "say something" at the funeral. What they say is often heartfelt praise and appreciation for the deceased, often expressed with deep emotion. Such opportunities may reveal an individual struggling with a deep sense of loss. These speeches can be cathartic for the speaker and the congregation. They often reveal sides of the deceased of which the preacher was unaware. They may also include flashes of humor that bring healing and delight. Our human condition is never more apparent than when we cry at weddings and laugh at funerals.

A preacher need not solicit such speakers, but when they offer themselves, whether directly or through an intermediary, they are hard to refuse, and probably there is no need. Theirs is a function different from that of the preacher. They are best understood as collaborators rather than competitors. Their words do not replace the sermon, but instead recall in very personal terms the life and death in question, and what the deceased means to the mourners. The memories, reflections, and bits of verse offered by these speakers help ground the entire liturgy, especially in settings where emotional restraint and good taste might otherwise reach unbearable proportions. What they have to contribute should be allowed to stand on its own, rather than be unnaturally incorporated into the sermon.

Perhaps the best place for such speakers is after the Gospel and before the sermon. This placement interrupts the flow directly from the Gospel to the sermon, but it seems more important that the sermon, with its emphasis on God's grace, have the last word after other addresses and be positioned to shed resurrection light on what has gone before. The aim of this placement is not to eliminate anything good and human, but to bring those very traits to their true fulfillment.

Sometimes a pastor may even decide to open the floor to anyone who wants to share a memory, although much care must be taken in discerning whether this is the appropriate thing to do. Opening the door in this way was successful at the funeral of an elderly woman who in her final years had become a free spirit who brought laughter and delight to those around her. The storytelling about her took on a life of its own, and it resembled the medieval practice of telling funny stories and jokes in church on the afternoon of Easter Day, to provide comic relief after the rigors of Lent. The storytelling at this woman's funeral did not distract from the sermon but perfectly set the stage for it.

↶ Use of the Key

Beyond all these considerations, the central issue for the sermon is making good use of the key. The key must be presented as what it is: something tangible and even ordinary, something whose validity will draw assent from every mourner present. The key must be something familiar that belongs directly or indirectly to the world where the deceased once lived.

After displaying the key in this way, the preacher must reveal how it suggests something so alive, so immediate, so irresistible as to be extraordinary—the gracious, saving activity of God. The preacher thereby reveals the congregation living in a world whose boundaries with a greater world are sometimes very thin indeed, perhaps even nonexistent. No series of instructions can ensure that the preacher will make this connection. It resides in the realm of poetry, not prose. The task is not to describe but to present, to give the congregation a vision not of facts but truth.

The preacher announces to the people: "Don't dismiss grace as something with which you have no experience! It shone and shimmered, however briefly, in the life that now is over. In that life you may recognize, however faintly, a cruciform pattern. Know then that grace will have its way, and that finally nothing good will be lost. There is a greater grace than any you've seen yet, so vast as to turn the Easter morning of Jesus into an outrageously universal resurrection."

The key must unlock the memories of those who listen, so that old scenes now bittersweet will be cause for gratitude as well as grief. The key will also unlock their hearts and begin to heal them from the pain, not only of this most recent death, but of all the deaths they have encountered before and all the deaths they fear in the future, including their own. Such unlockings as these are beyond unaided human capacity. The preacher must be content to surrender his or her words and voice to the Spirit of God.

⌣ Contemplative Perspective

Finding the key and constructing the sermon both require a contemplative stance in the face of time pressure and emotional demands. Both require an intentional listening. Finding the key requires listening to survivors and circumstances, noticing ordinary details and their extraordinary implications. The listening that underlies constructing the sermon is a more private process. The preacher prepares for this task by listening in the course of preparing other kinds of sermons and, above all, in the course of daily prayer. The preparation for preaching at a funeral thus starts well before the death occurs. Preparing the sermon means cultivating a contemplative perspective on everything, both what we call ordinary and what we deem extraordinary. It means recognizing that grace is at work in plain places. Most of all, it means believing that Easter is a way to see the future that is meant for one and for all.

⌁ Leading the Way Home

The funeral sermon is in a sense an epitome of all Christian ministry. For what has God called us to do but remind a world on its way to the grave of his overflowing grace and the resurrection open to all? We do not, need not, and can not pull people out of their funeral procession, but we *can* show them that really they are marching in a victory parade leading us all home.

A Selection of Sermons

A Feature of Our Common Humanity

WHEN OUR HANDS ARE EMPTY: HAROLD, NINETY YEARS OLD

The key used in this sermon is a feature of our common humanity: the emptiness of our hands when we enter and leave this world. Details of the life of the deceased came from his family and his obituary. The sermon opens with a touch of gentle humor as listeners are invited to imagine the nonagenarian they knew as he was on the day he was born.

Many of us are aware that this past Wednesday, two days ago, would have been Harold's ninety-first birthday. I invite us to go back in our imagination to a day none of us here is old enough to remember: May 28, 1905, the day Harold was born.

Perhaps you can imagine that birth. No doubt it was like what King Solomon tells us in the Book of Wisdom about the start of his own life: "When I was born, I came into the world like anyone else. I began to breathe the common air we all breathe; and like everyone else, the first sound I made was a cry. I was wrapped in cloths and cared for" (Wisdom 7:3–4).

This is how life begins. And there is another feature common to King Solomon and Harold, to you and to me: we all come into the world with empty hands.

Harold came into the world with empty hands, and through the decades of his life, he used these hands in many ways. His hands were busy at Ford Motor Company for forty years. At Fort Howes, Texas, his hands helped heal German prisoners who were far from the front line and far from home. Harold's hands built countless bird-houses and used small pieces of wood to craft intricate pictures. His hands held the hands of his wife, Muriel. His hands held young nieces and nephews—some of you here today—when you were small. His hands took hold of the Bread and Cup of Communion right at this altar.

Throughout his ninety years of life, Harold used his hands in many ways. Like all of us, he came into this world with empty hands. Those hands, that life, were filled with an abundance of blessings down through the years.

There were those simple blessings that we easily overlook: the green grass in the springtime, a neighbor's greeting on the sidewalk here in this town, the wind in your face as your motorboat cuts across the waves on Lake St. Clair.

And there were unusual, unique blessings. You who knew Harold and loved him are aware of these blessings and, I'm sure, you're thankful for them. Yes, Harold came into this world with empty hands, and into those hands, day by day, year by year, an abundance of blessings was placed. To that man an abundance of gifts was given.

He came into this world as a fresh, newborn baby at the opening of this century. Now he leaves this world as a ripe, mellow man, full of years, at the close of this century. And do you notice? He leaves as he came: with empty hands. There's a cartoon from *The New Yorker* magazine that shows two prosperous men looking out a window. Outside is a funeral procession making its way down the street. At the end of the line of cars there is an armored car. One of the men says to the other, "Well, I guess old Ponsonby *did* find a way to take it with him!" We smile at this because we know there's no way any of us can take it with us—whether 'it' is money or any of the blessings entrusted to us. We all leave this world with empty hands.

But the Gospel message is this—God is most free to work with us when our hands are empty.

Let's return to Harold. When he was born, back in 1905, when he arrived here with empty hands, God gave him an abundance of gifts. He came here with nothing. God gave him the substance of a unique and satisfying life. And in the process, God took a delightful baby and turned him into an even better treat: a delightful old man, someone able to speak a word of blessing to the people around him.

Do we dare think that God has given up on this long-term project of his that we know as Harold? He left this life with empty hands so that God could fill those hands with a plethora of new gifts, blessings beyond our ability to imagine, more than what is given in this life. For God is most free to work with us when our hands are empty.

Strange though it seems, it is when we have precisely nothing that the best things happen. When we are born into this world, we have nothing and yet we triumph gloriously: this entire world is God's gift. When we leave this world, we have even less, and yet we triumph all the more: God's gift is eternal life, the gift of life in all its fullness.

How do we know that God is most free to work with us when our hands are empty—even when our hands are empty in death? The cross teaches us this. For no hands are ever more empty than those of Jesus when pierced with nails. Yet Jesus is given new life. That is the gift placed in his hands. Not only for himself, but for the whole world—for Harold, you, and me. Jesus shares our death that we may share his life. His hands are empty in the grave that ours may be forever full. He is raised from death that we may live with him forever.

I remember once exploring another St. Paul's Episcopal Church—the one in Medina, Ohio. Like this one, it is located in a small, attractive town. There in the church, I came upon a memorial tablet honoring a Civil War soldier, Lt. Col. Herman Canfield, who died at the battle of Pittsburg Landing, Tennessee, at the age of forty-five. He was a man respected by his contemporaries. The memorial tablet describes him as, "A loving Husband, an affectionate Father, a worthy Citizen, an able Counselor, a wise Senator, and a faithful Soldier of the cross." The tablet also records that his dying words were, "A Christian need not fear to die."

A Christian need not fear to die.

That was the message of Herman Canfield's death for his contemporaries. That can be the message of Harold's death for us today. And it can be the wisdom with which each of us faces our own death whenever that happens.

A Christian need not fear to die.

We enter this world with empty hands, and we leave this world with empty hands. But here God fills our hands with gifts, and through Christ, he will do so even more abundantly in the life to come.

THE CARPENTER WILL COME: LILLIAN, AN OLDER WOMAN

The key to a funeral sermon may be an experience of the preacher's that occurs around the time of the death but is not directly related to it. This sermon, based on such an experience, uses the concrete, familiar image of a carpenter to portray the God who promises to resurrect the dead.

Yesterday afternoon, only a few hours after Lillian passed away, I went upstairs in my house to the master bedroom. What I saw there was devastation! The room was devoid of furnishings. The walls and ceiling had been gutted, leaving only an outward shell. In the middle of the floor was a huge pile of debris. Up in the ceiling electrical wires were visible, ancient wires that had not been seen since early in this century, when the house was built. The room was a wreck!

But this was what I had expected. For, you see, this devastation was not the result of some accident or natural disaster, nor had it been done by vandals. The wreckage I saw was the first step in the renovation and expansion of this room, the first step in a process that would result in a room more useful and beautiful than it had been before. And so I saw this devastation not as a permanent loss, but as a necessary stage on the way to something better. I had confidence that in due time the carpenter would come and that the new room would be a delightful place.

When a loved one dies, we may feel as though we are looking on a scene of devastation. Nothing is as it once was, and it will never be the same again. We face a choice. We can believe that devastation is the last word, and that nothing more will happen. Or we can believe that this devastation is not final, but is, in fact, a first step toward a renovation and expansion that will result in something even more useful, more beautiful, than what was there before. We can have confidence that the carpenter will come and set everything aright, and that the new room will be a delightful place.

Such was the case with Jesus. His execution on the cross was thorough devastation. His body was broken, his veins were emptied, his life ebbed out, and soon he was a corpse. Utter devastation, like a room reduced to wreckage.

That cold corpse was placed in a tomb, a boulder set to block the entrance, and those who mourned him thought everything was over. But God raised Jesus from the dead—more useful, more beautiful than before, a reason for rejoicing.

And God promises to raise us also; not as we once were, but renewed, renovated, made more useful, more beautiful, than ever before. We will be a delight, a reason for rejoicing for ourselves and each other, and for the God who finds pleasure in us.

A prayer later in this service, the prayer we call the Great Thanksgiving, expresses the confidence we can have. We will pray in these words: "For to your faithful people, O Lord, life is changed, not ended; and when our mortal body lies in death, there is prepared for us a dwelling place eternal in the heavens."[1]

"For to your faithful people, O Lord, life is changed, not ended; and when our mortal body lies in death, there is prepared for us a dwelling place eternal in the heavens."

And so this day, in the midst of our very real feelings of grief and loss, we offer thanks to God. We offer thanks for Lillian, for all she has meant to us, and all she continues to mean. We offer thanks for her devoted service as a kindergarten teacher, and for how she influenced for good so many hundreds of young lives. We offer thanks for the concern and love she showed over the years for her family, both those we see no longer and those gathered here today. And we offer thanks that what we face today is not a final devastation, but instead a first step toward a renovation and expansion that will make Lillian an even more useful, more beautiful, more delightful child of God than ever she was before.

We can have confidence that the carpenter will come and set everything right. "For to your faithful people, O Lord, life is changed, not ended; and when our mortal body lies in death, there is prepared for us a dwelling place eternal in the heavens."

---

1 Proper Preface for the Commemoration of the Dead, *The Book of Common Prayer*, p. 382.

OURSELVES AS THEIR MEMORIAL: JUSTIN AND RONALD, YOUNG BROTHERS KILLED IN A FIRE

Two little boys die in a house fire, and the ripples of grief touch an entire community. This sermon has for its key those gathered at the service, and specifically their outcry in the face of these deaths. This outcry is heard by God, whose own Son died and now lives forever, welcoming children as he did on earth. The mourners are invited to surpass their role as survivors, embody something of the boys' innocence and faith, and thus become their living memorial here on earth.

In this place today, there are many eyes wet with tears, and many hearts, yes, many hearts, heavy with sadness. Nor are we alone in the grief that brings us here today. Since Thursday, many other people have felt the hurt of what has happened. Many other eyes have been wet with tears. Many other hearts have been heavy with sadness. Firefighters and police officers and medical personnel and funeral home staff. Boy Scouts and members of the Moose lodge. Neighbors and friends, co-workers and acquaintances. People who listen to the news or read the paper, some of whom know what it is like from the inside to lose a child.

I'm not here to tell you that today you must dry your eyes. I'm not here to tell you that today the weight will be lifted from your heart. I'm not hear to tell you not to cry. For the tears in our eyes at a time like this are sacred. They are holy. They bear witness to your love for Justin, for Ronald, for members of their family.

It's been said that each of us faces two choices in life. We can have a broken heart, or we can have a shriveled heart. If you give yourself to anyone—a child, a spouse, a friend, a community—then sooner or later, your heart will break.

There's only one way to avoid a broken heart. That is to be careful never to give your heart away to anyone—not a child, a spouse, a friend, a community, or even an animal. Instead, store your heart away in some safe place, wrapped in small pleasures. But if you choose that, then something worse than a broken heart will happen. Your heart will shrivel. It will not be broken, but it will become dried up, desiccated, empty of love. Better that a heart be broken, so that love flows from it like rain moistening dry ground, than that a heart become shriveled and dry, with nothing to offer.[1]

We have this choice between a broken heart and a shriveled heart. Yet this is an assembly of the brokenhearted. You are here bearing witness to having given your hearts away. I am not here to tell you not to cry, but I am here to invite you to cry in a certain direction. Let me recall for you some of the history of tears.

The Israelites were slaves in Egypt, and their lot was going from terrible to even worse. The people of Israel groaned under their bondage. But they did not simply groan, they cried out. And their cry under bondage did not disappear on the wind. God heard their groaning. God heard them crying out. God remembered his covenant with their ancestors. God saw the people and knew their condition.

Today we feel a bondage, a bondage of grief that makes us groan, that makes us cry out. Know that our cry under this cruel oppression does not disappear on the wind. God hears our groaning, God hears our cry.

The prophet Jonah was cast into the sea and was swallowed up inside a huge fish. There in the dark, stinking belly of the fish, Jonah did not remain silent. Instead, he cried out! He cried out to the Lord. His cry did not disappear on the vast surface of the ocean. And God heard Jonah crying out from the dark, stinking belly of the fish.

It may be that grief has swallowed us, and we despair of seeing sunlight again, or breathing in clean air again. From inside this dark, stinking grief we cry out, and our cry does not disappear on the vast surface of the ocean. God hears our groaning, God heeds our cry.

The hands that healed the sick, fed the hungry, made the world—these hands were nailed to the cross. There on the cross, breathing out his life, bleeding out his blood, Jesus did not stay silent. He cried out to God—in fidelity, in trust, yet in deepest sorrow. And yes, God heard him. The proof came three days later.

It may be that the sorrow that brings us together today is killing something inside us, nailing us to a cross of deprivation and despair. We can cry out to God, and never fear that our voices will be lost on our personal Mount Calvary.

God heeds our groaning. God hears our cry.

What afflicts us is not shriveled hearts. We are better off than that. What afflicts us is broken hearts, shattered as though by a sledgehammer because of two terrible losses. And these broken hearts groan. They cry out. And they cry out not into an emptiness, but into the love of God.

Are you angry with God? Do you question God? Do you wonder if God is there? All good reasons to cry out, and then listen for an answer. Turn to the Psalms sometime, and you will find there many prayers in which the speaker argues with God, makes demands of God, screams out for help, questions the fidelity, challenges the justice of God. If it can happen in the Bible, it can happen in our lives. We can give voice to our broken hearts. God knows our raw emotions already; we need not fear to express them.

God is pure and powerful spirit. He is not made of fine china, easily shattered. Groan before God, cry out to him, expose before him your rawest, most unacceptable emotions, and you will find you do not threaten the divine. God is already broken, you see. God has a broken heart already. What more horrible loss can there be than to have your child die? Yet God knows this loss from the inside.

His child died on the cross, a death long and brutal and agonizing.

Christianity leaves no room for a god disconnected from the human condition, one who reigns on high, yet stays remote from our concerns. What Christmas means, what Christianity means, is that God knows this world of tears and death and sorrow, not as an observer, but from the inside, from the inside with a sensitivity that you and I cannot begin to imagine.

Jesus suffers death on the cross, and his Father suffers the agony of watching his Son die. Mary, the human parent of Jesus, has her heart pierced by a sword of grief on Calvary. Certainly then, a sword of grief pierces the heart of Jesus's other parent, his Father—and our Father—in heaven.

Death is strong. But God is stronger. Love finds a way, and divine love finds a way magnificently. The final word for Jesus is not tragedy, but new life. And the final word for Justin and Ronald is not tragedy, but new life in Jesus.

We need a picture of those two wonderful boys beyond their small caskets in this place, and we have that picture. It appears in the reading from Mark's Gospel we heard earlier in this service. There Jesus won't allow anybody to keep children away from him. He demands that they come to him unhindered so that he can take them up in his arms and, laying his hands on them, bestow on them a blessing.

During his life on earth, Jesus wouldn't allow anybody to keep children away from him. We can be sure that in his unending resurrection life he does not allow anyone or anything—not even death—to keep children away from him. As he once welcomed children of his native land, so today he welcomes Justin and Ronald, and they are safe with him.

We can be sure as well that those boys will speak to Jesus of those they love who are on earth. They will be good intercessors for their family and friends. We can keep them in our prayers as well, asking that they may continue to grow in the love of God.

The best memorial for these dear, beautiful children will not be something made from bronze or stone. It will be something alive. It will be us—their family, their friends, their neighbors. We will remember them best if we imitate their joy, these boys who were bundles of sunshine. We will honor them best by imitating their faith and innocence, for it is to children such as these that God's kingdom belongs.

To lay a foundation for ourselves as their memorial, let us rise, and cry out to God in hope, using the words of the prayer on the back of the service leaflet:

Merciful God, you grant to children an abundant entrance into your kingdom. In your compassion, comfort those who mourn for Ronald and Justin, and grant us grace to conform our lives to their innocence and faith, that at length, united with them, we may stand in your presence in the fullness of joy; for the sake of Jesus Christ. Amen.[2]

---

1 This passage is based on a description of the loveless heart in C. S. Lewis, *The Four Loves* (Harcourt, Brace & World, 1960), p. 169.
2 This prayer appears in *Enriching Our Worship 2* (Church Publishing, 2000), p. 144.

A Specific Characteristic of the Deceased

LIFE AS MUSIC:
IVA, LOVER OF MUSIC

The vocation or avocation of the deceased may provide a basis for proclaiming the Gospel of eternal life. In this sermon, an elderly woman's passion for music is connected with her eternal destiny, and both are connected with the listener's own life here and hereafter.

It's been said that music was her life. How true this is! There's proof in Iva's work as pianist in the schools of this city, in her service as organist of this parish, in the delight she found in music over the course of so many years. Yes, music was her life!

But this assertion leads to a question. Music ends. The sound disappears as soon as we hear it. Life ends. Our loved ones die and we see them no longer.

Is that all there is?

Christian faith tells us that the God who gives us life at our beginning also gives eternal life to everyone who will receive it. What we call the end of life is, in fact, the start of something greater.

The music we make here on earth—which passes away in a moment—is an anticipation of music that is unending, that flows forth forever; the music of worship, the sound of praise, the eternal alleluia.

All of Iva's existence—her years growing up; the life she lived in a house not far from here; her playing the piano in so many schoolrooms; her playing the organ at so many services; the quiet, simple years at the end of her life; all her frustrations and delights, all her troubles and joys—the entirety of Iva's existence was a rehearsal, a preparation for her part in that unending life, that unending music to which she was called early on Wednesday morning.

The same holds true for each of us. The things we do, the music we make, the succession of our days and months and years together constitute one vast rehearsal, preparation for a larger life and for a music that will never end.

This realization brings us face-to-face with a paradox. On the one hand, everything we do is of immense importance because it contributes to this rehearsal for eternal life and eternal song. Nothing is insignificant: not a single thought or word or action. Whatever we do is of immense importance.

At the same time, whatever we do now—however significant it may be—falls short of ultimate and final importance. What we do here is simply a rehearsal, marked, as rehearsals are, by imperfection, uncertainty, and incompleteness.

The music we make now finds its fulfillment only in the eternal music of that shining city to which each of us is called.

Because what we do here is of immense importance, but remains only the preparation for something greater, we can find for ourselves both meaning and mercy. We can live our lives as people who are both serious and playful. To be both serious and playful is the definition of a good musician. To be both serious and playful is also the definition of a good Christian.

Music was her life. This is true of Iva. It's also true of Iva and each of us that our life is a kind of music. Music that is in rehearsal, music that passes away, but nonetheless prepares us for a music that is larger and better and without any end. This other music is our lives brought to fulfillment: the sound of praise, the eternal alleluia.

MEMORIES AND HOPE
CHARLIE, WHO TOOK PRIDE IN HIS WORK

Items important to the deceased can be the starting points for relating that person's life to the hope we have in Christ. This sermon makes such use of a passport, a photograph, and a row of evergreens. It ends with a story of a holy death drawn from the subject's ethnic heritage.

All of us here today have memories of Charlie, memories that will grow ever more precious with the passage of time. I want to share with you several memories that I have of this man and relate them to the hope that is ours in Christ.

Being buried along with Charlie's body is his passport, the British passport that brought him to this country when he was only sixteen years of age. How well I remember him showing it to me! It is not an inconspicuous little booklet such as passports are today. No, it is a magnificent document that unfolds like a treasure map and features a picture of young Charlie. It marked the end of one period of his life and the start of another. It brought him from the Old World into the New World, and he always treasured it.

Charlie also brought with him from England another passport, one that he received at a tender age in a Yorkshire church. I mean his Baptism into the Christian faith. Through that Baptism he became "a member of Christ, the child of God, and an inheritor of the kingdom of heaven."

Charlie stopped traveling on his British passport many decades ago. But he never stopped traveling on his Baptismal passport, and he is traveling on that passport even now. We believe that he has entered more fully into that eternal life which became his through Baptism. And we believe that he will continue to increase in the knowledge and love of God, that he will never stop going from strength to strength in that life of perfect service which is God's kingdom.

I remember also a photograph he showed me of himself with the many men he supervised as a foreman at Goodyear. He was very proud of that photograph, and showed it to me several times. I never tired of seeing it, because I never tired of seeing the pleasure it gave him to show it to me!

Charlie was a man who took pride in his work, who was glad to have a man's job to do in the world. Ecclesiasticus, a book we Episcopalians include in the Apocrypha of the Bible, speaks of such men as him: "Without them the city would have no inhabitants; no settlers or travelers would come to it. They maintain the fabric of this world, and their daily work is their prayer" (Ecclesiasticus 38:32, 34). As he grew older, Charlie was pleased to see his son and his grandsons demonstrate their skillfulness.

Then, toward the close of his life, Charlie was called on to engage in a different sort of labor. He experienced pain and weakness and decreasing energy, certainly a hard trial for a man who loved to be active. In facing this, he participated in the suffering of Christ, and Christ participated in what happened to him.

We trust that as he suffered with Christ, so also will he be resurrected with Christ. Today we rejoice that Charlie so honorably completed the work of his lifetime, and that the suffering which once afflicted him is a thing of the past. Now nothing keeps him from the love of Christ, and his new work is praise.

Whenever I visited Charlie at his home, I would look at the gallant row of cedar trees that grow behind that house. Seeing them so tall and secure made me marvel that the man who planted them was there to tell the tale. Now it is the trees' turn to tell the tale. Unlike many trees in this area, these cedars do not lose leaves. They are always green. All the seasons of the year have their beauty, as so many trees break forth into bud, become green all over, change color, and finally lose their leaves. But there is a different kind of beauty in a tree that stays green, that remains unchanged throughout the seasons.

Charlie lived a long, rich life. Thirty-seven years' service at Goodyear. Sixty-four years of marriage to his beloved Florence. Nearly seventy years as an Akron resident. His life passed through all the seasons, and each season had a beauty of its own. But while the seasons have their beauty, that is not the whole story.

Like every one of us, Charlie is meant to be an evergreen, one whose witness to life is unbroken. Today that is our prayer and our hope.

Charlie was a man who never forgot his English roots. And so I want to conclude with the story of another son of England, one who was both a king and a saint, namely Edward the Confessor.

This Edward was many things, and he was certainly a builder. Almost a thousand years ago he was responsible for the first Westminster Abbey, a church of chiseled stone and carved wood and painted glass such as England had never seen before. Throughout fifteen years the king watched the abbey being built. Gradually his strength declined, and the veil separating him from the next life grew thinner and thinner. At last the end came, and he spoke his final words. "Weep not," he said, "I go from the land of the dead to the land of the living."[1]

I daresay that Charlie would like to place a hand on the shoulder of each of us and say that. "Weep not. I go from the land of the dead to the land of the living."

---

1 H. F. B. Mackay, *Followers in the Way* (New York: Macmillan, 1934), pp. 93–96.

FOR GEAN, EASTER CAME EARLY:
A WOMAN WHO DIED AFTER A LONG ILLNESS

Sometimes the key for a funeral sermon comes from circumstances around the death. Gean died a couple of weeks before Easter, and so entered Easter early after a long illness that was her own private Lent. A foretaste of that Easter was apparent in the jubilation people noticed in her shortly before she died.

We are gathered here today as relatives and friends of Gean to vent our grief and also to express our gratitude. Grief at our loss, at the empty space in our lives. Gratitude for everything Gean's meant to us, and everything she continues to mean. It is a day for tears and smiles.

Each life that intersects with our own can bring us some awareness of God, whether through that person or despite that person. Gean gave us reminders of God through the person she was. She bore witness to the truth through her humor, her art, her cooking, her love of family, and her willingness—what a gift it was—her willingness simply to be herself. For these reasons, and others as well, we can offer thanks today, though it be through our tears.

Gean was a Christian, an Episcopalian, and she wore an enamel pin with the red, white, and blue shield of the Episcopal Church. In recent years she was rarely able to attend public worship, yet she remained vitally connected with the Church through prayer and regular reception of the Blessed Sacrament.

And so there was something appropriate, something liturgical, about the time of year that Gean's death occurred. It was in Lent, the period of preparation that leads to Easter. I've been told that Easter was Gean's favorite season. The rest of us still have a ways to go before the arrival of this year's Easter: tomorrow and the next day and all next week stand between us and that festival. But for Gean, Easter came early.

On March 19, I visited Gean and gave her her last communion. As she and Lowell and I sat in a small circle in the living room of the house where she was born, I had no idea that this would be her last communion, her *viaticum*, her provision for the journey into eternal life that would soon take place.

Yet there was something extraordinary about that visit which I noticed even then. From the moment I saw Gean, I could see that she was jubilant. Our subsequent conversation revealed nothing to account for this jubilation, though I continued to sense it throughout that visit.

Others who visited Gean in the last days of her life have also said that she seemed unexpectedly jubilant, more joyous than she had appeared for years. I wonder: Did she know something then, something the rest of us would never have guessed?

Perhaps she took delight at the prospect of departing this life, of setting aside her illness, of leaving the town and the house where she had lived so long and taking up residence in her heavenly Father's home, "that place where there is no pain or grief, but life eternal." I can't say what she knew or did not know. But there was this jubilation near the end. Perhaps she knew that, for her, Easter would come early.

Gean had an agile sense of humor. She may have been amused that for her Easter came early this year, while the rest of us remain to plod our way through the final days of Lent. Maybe there is a certain justice that for her Easter came early. Her illness constituted a lengthy private Lent—a time marked by struggle, desolation, and emptiness. Yet Lent, even so strict a Lent as that, is never for its own sake. We are emptied so that we may be filled with divine life. Lent was not to be the last moment for Gean. For her, Easter came early this year, an eternal Easter.

At this service Gean shares with us the gift she received of an early Easter. Although April 12 is still in the future, for today at least Lent's "long shadows have departed," the purple hangings and vestments are nowhere to be seen, and Alleluia sounds forth in this church. The liturgy we offer at her burial is an Easter liturgy.

Through scripture and song, prayer and action, we demonstrate our belief that, for Gean, Easter came early. We share with her in that eternal Easter. The risen Christ welcomes her to her new home. We meet him also in the word proclaimed, the community gathered, in bread and wine offered and received. Her Christ is our Christ. And so, while we see her never again in this life, we remain with her still in the commonwealth of divine love.

Easter came early for Gean, and it is hers forever. This morning we share in that Easter and look forward to when it will be ours forever.

GRIEF AND GRATITUDE:
CHARLES, WHO HAD A TROUBLED LIFE

A person dies who is widely known for having made a wreck of life. Is it possible to bear witness to grace at work in such a sad story? Sometimes the congregation can be called upon to search their memories and find God's fingerprints on the life of that troubled person. This sermon describes a means of doing so.

When a death occurs and a memorial service is held, there's a way in which the universal and the particular come together. The person who has died is one particular person—with a name, a face, a life story. Yet at the same time, the dead one is not simply a single individual, but somehow represents each of us, frail creatures of flesh. The poet-preacher John Donne put it in this way, "Any man's death diminishes me, because I am involved in Mankind; and therefore never send to know for whom the bell tolls; it tolls for thee."[1]

Let me speak first about the universal: what Charles shares with every member of the human race.

He was fashioned by the hands of God and given the breath of life. At the center of his being there was what scripture calls the image of God, the divine reflection in our human existence.

That heavenly image was disfigured by sin as it is disfigured in each of us. And as suffering lays a hand on each of us, so too did Charles know that experience in ways both large and small. Then what happens to each of us someday happened to him last week—he passed through the gate of death.

But human nature has been united to the divine in Jesus Christ; through Christ's humanity, ours is redeemed. And so we gather this night in confidence that death is not the final word for Charles or for any of us. God has made a covenant with us, and God is ever faithful.

There is nothing created which Christ has not redeemed. There is no place where he is not king, and so we can boldly pray this ancient prayer for Charles, for ourselves, and for all people, "Of old you created me from nothing, and honored me with your divine image; but when I disobeyed your commandment, you returned me to the earth whence I was taken. Lead me back again to your likeness, refashioning my ancient beauty."[2]

Such is the universal story. Now comes the particular. This, dear friends, is your province rather than mine. Some among you lived with Charles in the intimacy of family life. Others among you worked on the same campus with him. Still others were his neighbors here in this community. You know the unique features of his story. You lived that story with him. The loss you have suffered leaves you grieving. A part of you has died as well. But I invite you to find, at the still center of your grief, the gratitude that waits there to be discovered again.

After I finish speaking, you will have opportunity to express your gratitude for Charles. There's a blank paper in your service bulletin. Pencils will be made available. You will have the chance to write down something about Charles's life for which you want to thank God. Some experience you shared with him. An act of kindness that he did. Something he taught you. An occasion when he forgave you. Perhaps that something comes immediately to mind. Or it may be that you search in memory's closet for some treasure wrapped up and stored away long years ago. You may have many reasons for gratitude, but for now focus on only one, one that is concrete.

Write down that reason for gratitude, and feel free in doing so. No one will ever read your words. Your papers will be burnt in my fireplace at home. Burning is, after all, a reverent way to dispose of anything sacred: old altar cloths, vestments that are worn out, even the human body once life has left it.

Once the papers have been collected, we'll sing a hymn, one familiar to many people, "Now thank we all our God." This hymn is frequently sung at the Thanksgiving holiday. It's bright and cheerful, a song for a sunlit morning, not the obvious choice for a nighttime memorial service. But let me introduce the author of this hymn, Martin Rinckart, a pastor in seventeenth-century Germany.

The greater part of this man's pastoral career took place amid the horrors of the Thirty Years' War. His hometown became a refuge for fugitives, and the overcrowding resulted in pestilence. For some time Rinckart was the only clergyman in the place. Often he read the burial service for more than fifty people in one day. During the pestilence he buried more than four thousand people in all.[3]

Yet it was this man, haunted by grief, who wrote a

hymn that has survived the centuries as a statement of gratitude. My hope is that each of us will discover our gratitude and give expression to it here in the midst of our grief. May it be so!

1 Meditation XVII.
2 From the funeral service of the Orthodox Church.
3 James Mearns in John Julian, ed., *A Dictionary of Hymnology*, 2nd rev. ed. (New York: Dover Publications, 1957), pp. 962–63.

THE INTIMACY OF HOME

A FAMILY MAN:
TOM, A BELOVED GRANDFATHER

Sometimes it becomes wonderfully apparent that the deceased found his or her vocation and faithfully fulfilled it. Such was the case with the man profiled in this sermon, whose care for his family left them with a precious legacy, and offered to all who knew him a reminder of that greater family to which he was called home.

I would like to begin this sermon in an unusual way. Please take *The Book of Common Prayer* and turn to page 828. At the bottom of that page there appears a prayer entitled "For Families." Reading aloud together, let us offer that prayer.

> Almighty God, our heavenly Father, who settest the solitary in families: We commend to thy continual care the homes in which thy people dwell. Put far from them, we beseech thee, every root of bitterness, the desire of vainglory, and the pride of life. Fill them with faith, virtue, knowledge, temperance, patience, godliness. Knit together in constant affection those who, in holy wedlock, have been made one flesh. Turn the hearts of the parents to the children, and the hearts of the children to the parents; and so enkindle fervent charity among us

all, that we may evermore be kindly affectioned one to another; through Jesus Christ our Lord. *Amen.*

Tom was a member of the Episcopal Church, a long-time, faithful member. No doubt there were times when he prayed that prayer in public worship or his private devotions. But more than that, he lived this prayer with his life. It was his life.

Tom was something wonderful and all too rare. He was a family man. In his quiet, persistent, steadfast way, he was committed to his wife, his daughters and their husbands, and his grandchildren. This commitment was the music of his life throughout the nearly fifty years since he and Margaret were married here at Grace Church.

We could talk about Tom's work in drugstores of this community and in a local hospital. We could talk about young Tom's bravery during the Second World War and the medal that he won. We could talk about the friendly welcome he gave as an usher in this church and wherever there was anyone for him to meet. We could talk about all these things and more, and those of us with stories about Tom should share them today and in days to come. But we would miss the essence of this man if we did not recognize—and thank God for it!—that Tom was a family man.

He made it look easy. Popcorn with the kids. Going out on a summer morning, a smile on his face, eager to do errands that would lighten someone else's load. He made it look easy. The religious word for this is vocation. Vocation is when you find what you're here to do, and you do it, and regardless of the inevitable mistakes and rough moments, you find in what you do a deep joy, a satisfaction, as though God intends this role just for you, which is, of course, the case. God does intend it this way.

Tom found his vocation, and responded to it with fidelity. He found deep joy in what he did and who he was, and that joy was contagious. People around him caught on to it, and were made that much more joyous by his joy.

It's been said that some people make headlines, and others make history. Tom did not make headlines; his name was not often in the paper. Yet he made something more important. He made history. That history is written in the lives of countless people in this community and of those of us gathered here this morning. Above all that history is written in the lives of Tom's family. It is there that he leaves a legacy that exceeds all price, and it is for this legacy that we give thanks today.

Yet today is also an occasion of grief. Tom was a family man. This means he was present to his loved ones, truly present to them, involved in their lives. And because that presence was so precious, his absence is keenly felt. As the love is great, so too is the grief.

The Christian response is not to deny this grief, but to assert that it can coexist with hope. My friends, do not grieve as those without hope! Grieve because you must; it is right and proper so to do. The tears are holy; they testify to your love. But grieve and hope at once.

Grieve, because of the loss of Tom's immediate presence; grieve because of the absence and the emptiness. But hope as well, hope because the parting is not permanent. The one you now look for in vain you will see again when you both inhabit that larger, greater life. Hope because you believe in the resurrection of Jesus and the resurrection of all who belong to him.

Tom was a family man. He remains a family man still. The man you knew belonged not only to those united to him by blood and marriage, he belonged also to another family: the family of God's people. God sets the solitary in families in homes here on earth, homes which are meant to be havens of blessing and peace. And at the end, God welcomes us home to that larger family which includes all his people.

We believe that God welcomes Tom home as a son, a son who was a faithful Christian and a family man. Scripture tells the story of how one son was welcomed home, someone far less reliable than Tom. For this prodigal the fatted calf was killed and roasted, there was music and dancing, everybody in town was invited, and the guy was dressed up in a sharp suit and a fancy ring. For Tom there will be all that—all that, and popcorn too.

HER PLACE WAS THE HOME: PHLINDA, A MAKER OF MEMORIES

Some people live very private lives yet make a tremendous contribution to the world through their families. Building on memories of home life can produce an effective sermon and remind us that happy experiences of an earthly home prepare us for our final home, the new Jerusalem.

Phlinda's life fit neatly inside the twentieth century. She was born when this century was still new. She leaves us when this century is almost over. Phlinda's life fit neatly inside this span of time.

Phlinda's life also fit neatly inside another span. A span not of time, but of space, affection, relationships, activities. Her place was the home. It is there that she fit so well. That is where she spent herself, and found her life, and gave it to others.

Some people find their place in the wide world, but Phlinda's way, no less an adventure, was to find her place at home. At the risk of redundancy, let me say that it was at home that she found herself at home, and she welcomed others there.

Some of us here today remember that welcome and delight in those memories. The bountiful store of treats she offered to her grandchildren: circus peanuts, pink mints, popcorn, Vargo pop, and all the rest. Watching Bonanza. Watching Lawrence Welk. The great meals. She made even beans taste exceptional. The Christmas wrapping so perfect you hardly dared to tear through to the gift inside. Sheets ironed, and even socks ironed!

Such a sense of home as memories are made of. Home was Phlinda's place. She fit in well there and offered a welcome to others, among them adults who found in her the grandmother they had been waiting for.

Phlinda's life fit inside the span of this century and the span that we call home, a span of space, affection, relationships, activities. But that old home is no more. Did it bear fruit? Does it bear fruit still?

Some leave behind them institutions, works of intellect or imagination, achievements recorded where all can read. Not so Phlinda. Her accomplishments were private, personal. But did her life bear fruit? Of course it did! Look around you today at her children and grandchildren and her grandchildren's children. Look beyond them to the lives she touches through them. It's a secret harvest, yet a bountiful one. Hers was a domestic life, yet she leaves her legacy across the wide world. She proves true what Henry Ward Beecher once said, "Whoever makes home seem to the young dearer and more happy, is a public benefactor."

"Whoever makes home seem to the young dearer and more happy, is a public benefactor." So call this woman a public benefactor, but I will call her something else as well. I call her a teacher of theology, a preacher, an evangelist. She leaves painted in the memory of those she loved such a picture of home that they long for that home which no one reaches this side of heaven.

The comfort of a grandmother's house gains a place in the memory and imagination of a child, and prepares that child to welcome a vision of heaven. Circus peanuts and pink mints set the stage for other kinds of manna. Christmas presents so perfectly wrapped point the way to even more beautiful gifts.

The glad old hymn is correct which sings of "Jerusalem, my happy home." For heaven is a home, a place of Sabbath rest. The joys of earthly homes are but a first taste. Happy are those who know such earthly joys as prepare them for the joys of heaven!

Dear old Phlinda was only hours from her end when

I saw her smile and laugh as someone roundly amused, not only at the banter of her grandson, but at a certain unseen, cosmic humor.

I believe she died amused at the whole thing. Amused at life and death and the life to come. She left this world alive with Easter laughter. Her eyes sparkled with awareness of a great reversal. The old lady had spent her life at home, had given herself to others by offering them a home. Now she found that she was on the road, heading home. It was someone else's turn to hand out the treats.

Maybe that was what she smiled about in her final hours as she held on to a little olive wood cross as though it was her passport. That she, after almost a century of life, was about to be ushered in by Christ and welcomed home as a beloved child.

Perhaps that is what she was laughing about, and why she is laughing still.

The Deceased as a Mirror of Christ

SERVICE AND CONTEMPLATION:
HELEN, WHO PUT HER FAITH TO WORK

Christ can become visible through someone's voluntary service to others. This person's emblem is the towel Jesus picks up after the Last Supper. Voluntary service may be the outgrowth of a different, less obvious, aspect of character: a contemplative dimension that finds God present throughout the world, and reaches its fulfillment on the other side of death.

Every one of us, I suppose, has our mental pictures of Helen, memories that live in our hearts. In one of mine, I see her at the opposite end of this room on a Sunday morning, in an attractive outfit, complete with a small hat, and eager to welcome those who have come to church. In my picture, Helen is the consummate church greeter: a pleasant, hospitable person, who makes everyone who walks through the doors feel at home.

It was only for ten years that I had the privilege of knowing Helen here on earth. Some of us gathered this morning have known her far longer. But I'm aware of enough of her history to recognize that my picture of Helen greeting people here at St. Paul's catches something essential about her. So much of her life was welcoming people, offering hospitality, extending help to those who needed it. I'm sure that in all the places she did so, she offered her service with the same understated and highly effective grace that she demonstrated at this church.

Consider several of the ways Helen was of service to people known to her and unknown. She worked for more than a decade at Sperry's, that Port Huron landmark. There's a certain curious synchronicity to how Sperry's closing and Helen's leaving us occurred within a year or so of each other. For me, both the woman and the store stand as symbols of a gentler, more genteel age, and our city is much the poorer for having had to say goodbye to both.

I can picture Helen there at Sperry's, being of service to her neighbors. I can picture her also helping her neighbors as a member of the Port Huron Hospital Auxiliary, though it surpasses my ability to imagine her half century of service. Consider that, my friends—five decades, fifty years, more than eight thousand hours. Nowadays we change commitments often, we complain of burnout, we crave novelty, but for half a century Helen stood faithful, helping her neighbors at some of their most difficult moments.

The same holds true for her service with the St. Clair County chapters of both the American Cancer Society and the March of Dimes. There she did not necessarily see the people she was helping, but that did not deter her. Still Helen stood by, extending herself, helping her neighbor.

There's a way in which every faithful Christian reflects something of the reality of Christ, some facet of Jesus still at work in this world. Meditating on Helen's life and witness, I am reminded of one picture of Jesus that occurred on the night before his death. In St. John's Gospel, we read that following the Last Supper, Jesus rose from the table, took a towel, poured water into a basin, and began to wash his disciples' feet. His disciples were shocked by this action. It was a surprise to them. Certainly it was not something he was expected to do.

As with Jesus, so with Helen. Much that she did she did not have to do, but she chose to do. She could have worked at Sperry's without being as thoroughly gracious as she was. No one would have objected if she had chosen not to be a greeter, or a hospital volunteer for a half century, or if she had chosen not to serve with the American Cancer Society or the March of Dimes. She decided to serve in those ways, and she did so with a special grace.

Thus when I picture her greeting people at the church door, I imagine her in an attractive outfit, complete with a small hat. But I guess I also see her holding the towel of service that Jesus picked up after the Last Supper.

There's another aspect to Helen's life that I want to mention. It complements the service that she offered so readily and so well. Indeed, I see it as the source of Helen's long-term willingness to help her neighbors. From what I knew of her, I would say that Helen was something of a contemplative. Now if I had ever told her that I considered her a contemplative, she probably would have smiled, softly chuckled, and adroitly changed the subject.

But a contemplative she was. She saw beyond the ordinary, the everyday, the mundane, to recognize what is extraordinary, what is gracious, what is holy. Or to put it more accurately, she saw through the ordinary, the everyday, the mundane, to recognize their true character as extraordinary, gracious, and holy. She loved natural beauty because to her the beauties of nature bore their eloquent witness to their Creator. This contemplative vision was, I believe, a natural endowment, yet also something she kept alive and put to use throughout her lifetime.

Helen was somebody who put her faith to work through helping others. Yet I think she would also endorse a definition of religion I distributed to my World Religions class yesterday. This definition comes from Alfred North Whitehead, a philosopher whose later life overlapped with Helen's early years. Describing religion as a vision, Whitehead says that "religion is the vision of something which stands beyond, behind, and within the passing flux of immediate things; something which is real, and yet waiting to be realized; something which is a remote possibility, and yet the greatest of present facts."[1]

It seems to me that Helen caught this vision Whitehead describes, and never lost it. It became for her the basis for serving her neighbors over many years in a variety of settings, and doing so with care and grace and style. For who she was and what she did and the example she offers us we have cause to offer abundant thanks.

Now she has gone on to enjoy the vision of God which for her is no longer veiled by the passing flux of earthly things. She needs to wait no longer, for what is real, truly real, is the inheritance she has gone to receive. No longer is eternal life a remote possibility. It is for her a truth rich with delight.

It is necessary for us to mourn our loss, for we are made poorer by Helen's absence from us. Yet we can also rejoice. For Helen hears from Christ a hearty "Well done!" for her service to her neighbors, and her contemplative desire for God now knows its fulfillment. Her new life in the kingdom will be what St. Augustine so aptly describes, "There we shall rest and we shall see; we shall see and we shall love; we shall love and we shall praise. Behold, what shall be in the end, and shall not end!"[2]

---

1 Quoted in Richard H. Rupp, ed., *Critics on Emily Dickinson* (University of Miami Press, 1972), p. 124.

2 *The City of God*, Book 22, chapter 30.

PASSION AND RESURRECTION: SHARON, A YOUNG WOMAN WHO DIED AFTER A LONG ILLNESS

The Christian pattern is to die and rise with Christ. Our resurrection depends on his, and our suffering is a sharing in his own. The image of each Christian as another Jesus, crucified yet triumphant, comes out with particular force in the case of Sharon, who, after a lengthy illness, died at the same age as Jesus: thirty-three.

Each of us has memories of Sharon, memories that we treasure and find significant. I hope that we will share with each other these valuable memories in the hours ahead and in the years to come.

One memory of Sharon that I have recalls her presence at St. Paul's Church last Palm Sunday. It is the final time I remember seeing Sharon there, and since her death, that appearance has taken on increasing significance for me.

Palm Sunday actually has two names. The other name is the Sunday of the Passion. The Sunday of the Passion—because on this particular Sunday, the Passion, the story of the suffering and death of Jesus, is recounted word by word from the New Testament. The story is a long one, and it is our custom to read it dramatically, with members of our parish taking the different parts.

So there Sharon was, on a Sunday only a few months ago, caught up in the story of how Jesus spent the last week of his life on earth and died a human death at the age of thirty-three.

Today we face the horrible fact that Sharon also died her human death at the age of thirty-three. There is something severe and grievous about it all that makes the platitudes often spoken in a place like this so singularly inappropriate. We are not talking about someone who leaves this life after eighty or ninety years, whose children have gray hair and whose sturdy grandchildren serve as pallbearers. What we have instead is someone who dies at an age younger than most of us who mourn her, who leaves behind young children—dear, tender, delightful daughters who deserve and need something better than this. What we have is someone cut down in life's summertime, and anybody with even half a heart is left with heavy grief. Returning home from this place yesterday, I found that my driving was inattentive, distracted, almost dangerous.

In this sea of grief we look around for an island of significance, a rock of meaning. Perhaps we can find this for ourselves if we consider again the death of that other thirty-three-year-old which is told in the Passion story.

If ever anyone died innocent, he is the one. The survivors he leaves behind are almost broken by their grief. For he who was Life—their own life, and the life of all who live—now rests cold and dead on the burial slab. Now the entire world appears to be winter—frigid, heartless, eternal winter.

The wonder of it is that at the cold center of this winter landscape, at the hopeless midnight of this frigid darkness, there bursts into blossom a flower never seen before. The beloved rises to life—not the same life as before, but something better—the fullness of life, a new life that is unconquerable and unending.

This fresh flower, bursting forth to life and brilliance in the winter darkness of our cold world, stands as the promise of an unexpected springtime. The beloved one, comes forth from his place of burial, is the first of a countless number to pass from death to a life that is unconquerable, unending. The Passion story seems to reach its conclusion at the tomb. What it does is turn a corner, a corner beyond our ability to imagine, that leads to the shining city, the new Jerusalem, where at last our tears will be dried.

We come this morning with hearts full to the brim with grief, but yet as people who hold fast to hope—a hope so strange that it seems like a blossom bright and beautiful against the winter darkness.

Sharon has had her Sunday of the Passion. We trust that now she enters her Day of Resurrection, her eternal Easter, the life unending and unconquerable. That life is our final hope, and will be our great delight.

BRIAN WILL LIKE IT THERE:
A NONCHURCHGOING MAN,
BUT NO STRANGER TO GRACE

When the seed of grace is allowed to grow, each of the baptized comes to reflect Christ in certain distinct ways. Brian mirrored Christ in several respects, particularly in a love for children that placed him in the tradition of Celtic Christianity. The sermon closes with a surprising view of the renewed and restored Jerusalem.

I stand before you today to speak of a man that many of you know well. He was gifted with an ironic sense of humor. He was actively involved in the lives of countless children. He liked to mix with people of all sorts, with anyone who would accept him for who he was. He helped people who needed help, and did so simply, without fanfare. This was a man who enjoyed working with his hands, and what he built from wood was of benefit to the people around him.

Who is this man I am talking about? It sounds like Brian, doesn't it? Yet it also sounds like someone else. It sounds like Jesus. Gifted with an ironic sense of humor. Actively involved in the lives of children. Mixing with people of every kind. Helping those in need. Someone with a knack for carpentry. There are resemblances, to be sure. It is an intriguing thing, how in each of those baptized into Christ, where the seed of grace is allowed to grow, the person comes to reflect Christ in certain distinct ways. Each one of the baptized becomes, as it were, a facet of the mystery of Christ.

We gather this day for a cluster of reasons. We are here to share the grief that hangs heavy on our hearts, to give expression to that grief, and so make the burden more bearable.

We are here also to thank God for Brian's life and influence—for all he meant to us, and all he continues to mean. We join in prayer this day, not only for ourselves, but for Brian also, that this man who struggled through a long illness may now rest with all the saints in the eternal habitations.

Finally, we resort to the altar to receive solace and strength and to realize that our relationship with Brian has not been abolished but has assumed a new form, for to the people of God life is changed, not ended.

Brian loved a joke; he loved a funny story. Now it seems the best laugh of all that this man, perhaps entirely without knowing it, painted us a portrait of Christ in so many aspects of his life. He would, no doubt, blush at the very suggestion of this, and deny it vehemently, but this may well be the delightful trick that God played on him: to make him reflect something of Christ, to make him a saint of the best and most unconventional sort.

Brian had an ironic sense of humor. The gospel stories of Jesus are full of irony. He warns the judgmental to pull out the tree trunk from their own eyes before searching for the speck in somebody else's.

Brian was actively involved in the lives of children, not only Lynn and Michael, but crowds of other kids in Little League and Babe Ruth baseball, in the neighborhood, and who knows where else. There are plenty of adults in this community who are better people because of his influence when they were kids.

Jesus also took a practical interest in the lives of children. They responded to him naturally. His disciples saw these kids as a nuisance and tried to intervene, but Jesus told these disciples to shove off, and indicated these kids, straight from the streets, were closer to the kingdom of God than they were. It's not hard to imagine Brian delivering a line like that.

Brian liked to mix with people of all kinds, at least those who would accept him for who he was. In recent years his place for doing this was a certain doughnut shop over on Pine Grove Avenue. There he practiced an art that is unfortunately neglected in our society—he hung out, enjoying the company of other people. And he would help them, so far as they had need and he had ability. He did this without fanfare.

Jesus lived in a society where different groups of people were separate from one another, but he violated the boundaries. He would gladly spend time with anyone who would accept him, and even some who didn't. It was a doughnut shop approach to life.

Brian enjoyed working with his hands, and some of us here today are beneficiaries of his skill at carpentry and landscaping. Jesus was a builder by trade; it was the trade Joseph taught him. Both Jesus and Brian were willing to take their share in the toil of the world and make that work a source of satisfaction and a way of self-offering.

In recent years, there has been renewed interest in what is called Celtic Christianity. This refers to the spirituality of the ancient churches in the various Celtic lands, including Ireland, Scotland, and Wales. It is a spirituality associated with such saints as Patrick and David, Brigid and Hilda. This spirituality remains an important feature in modern churches of several denominations, and in some places it is a significant cultural factor.

Given his full name, it's safe to say that Brian was of Celtic ancestry. Certainly his spirituality had a Celtic flavor. One way in which this was apparent was in his love for children. A high regard for children is a prominent theme in Celtic spirituality. The early Celtic Christians believed that there was a certain wisdom to be found in children, at least in those children still free enough to be themselves. These children have something to teach those of us who are grown up. Through their example they can help us discard false lessons of adulthood and bring us a little closer to the kingdom of God. It seems that Brian had awareness of this wisdom and knew he was not only giving something to kids, but was being blessed by them as well.

One picture that the Bible gives us of heaven is that it is a city. John's Revelation describes this city in stately terms: the new Jerusalem coming down out of heaven from God, having the glory of God, its radiance like a most rare jewel, like a jasper, clear as crystal. The city stands foursquare, with three gates of pearl on each side, and the streets are of gold.

The prophet Zechariah augments this picture. He too speaks of a Jerusalem renewed and restored, and he adds one detail that I always find strangely moving. He says that on that holy mountain, in that faithful city, the streets will be full of boys and girls at play.

I think that Brian will like it there.

THE DECEASED AS ONE
RESPONDING TO GOD

SHADOW OF THE FATHER:
JOSEPH, A RELIABLE DAD

The saints of scripture and church history represent a continuation and manifestation of Christ's resurrection victory over the forces of death. A Christian's resemblance to one of these saints is, therefore, an aspect of that Christian's unique showing forth of Christ. Here the key was recognizing that a man named Joe had more in common with the foster father of Jesus than simply his name.

Something that happens in families, especially large ones, is that people look for family resemblances. A child, a grandchild, a great-grandchild somehow resembles an earlier member of the family in appearance, character, or life story. A younger person is said to have someone else's nose or eyes, or to have inherited her grandmother's voice or her aunt's eccentricity, or to have followed the path of his elder brother. This is what happens in families, especially large ones. We look for resemblances, and frequently we find them.

The Christian Church is a family, a very large one when we consider how it extends mightily through the centuries and across the globe. And occasionally in the Church we discover a family resemblance even when we are not looking to find one.

Some of us here today have known Joe for a very long time: perhaps from when he was a kid in grammar school, or when he married Grace at the age of twenty, or when the two of them were surrounded by a flock of fine young children.

My memory of Joe goes back only ten years, but I feel that during that time he and I became pretty well acquainted. And somewhere along the way the realization dawned on me that there was a resemblance between the Joe I knew and somebody else in the Christian Church. I was not looking to find this resemblance, but I guess it found me.

Maybe it was the name they shared that sparked my recognition of this resemblance; the name, plus how each man was skilled in carpentry. For you see, the resemblance that came to my attention was between this Joe and St. Joseph, the husband of Mary and foster father of Jesus. Remember what I told you—I did not go looking for this resemblance. It came looking for me.

The more I came to know Joe, and experienced him passing through phases of his life, the more I saw him come to terms with grief and grow in Christian commitment and spiritual depth, the more I could not shake this sense that here was a family resemblance between one guy named Joseph and another, though at least one of them preferred to be called Joe.

I tell you this, and I tell it to you on this occasion, because I think it may help us recognize better how God's grace was at work in the earthly life of the man whose Easter liturgy we celebrate today.

Let us consider then the New Testament Joseph. Let's look past the manger scene ornament to consider the real man of flesh and blood, fears and joys, as we find him in the pages of scripture.

When we do this, what we find is that Joseph, the husband of Mary and foster father of Jesus, makes just a few appearances. With but one exception, he turns up as a character only in the stories around the conception and birth of Jesus. That one exception is when, at the age of twelve, Jesus has a field day in the temple while Joseph and Mary are at their wits' end trying to find him.

Joseph doesn't appear in stories about the adult Jesus, even though Mary does. The usual assumption is that Mary was left a widow sometime between when Jesus was twelve and when he began his public ministry.

Something else about those times when Joseph appears in the New Testament. He never gets a line. No, not one. We hear about who he is, what he does, and what's been happening around him, but we have not one word from his lips.

Yet, despite this silence and these few references, we do gain a sense of the man and his character. We can paint a convincing portrait of Joseph as a hardworking laborer concerned for his family and choosing, even at great risk, to follow God's will for him. His faith is put to the test more than once, and he remains obedient to God, responsive to God.

Something more about the New Testament Joseph— he and Mary are entrusted with caring for Jesus, protecting him, nurturing him, and modeling for him what it means to be an adult. It's like a lightning bolt when we consider it, my friends. Joseph was the man closest to Jesus during our Lord's formative years. More than any other man, Joseph influenced the human character of Jesus.

It's rightly said that a child's first models for God are his or her parents. If so, then Joseph was a divinely ordained instrument to help Jesus the baby, the child, and the twelve-year-old to reflect the character of his Father in heaven. Andrew Doze's book about this man has an entirely appropriate title, *Saint Joseph: Shadow of the Father.*

What's remarkable about all this is that Joseph is not a guy in the spotlight. He works in the background. He's not sensational, but he's reliable. He doesn't make waves, but he makes a difference. St. Joseph is a good man, and a good father. He is indeed a treasure.

With obvious exceptions, this sketch of St. Joseph sounds a lot like our Joe as I came to know him over the last ten years. Joe was a quiet guy. He did not attract the spotlight. Yet, more importantly, he was a hardworking man, concerned for his family, and wanting always to follow God's will for him.

Joe worked in the background. He was not sensational, but he was reliable. He did not make waves, but he made a difference. And Joe was a father. He was a father to children and grandchildren. And as St. Joseph's fatherhood of Jesus was not biological, so our Joe did not limit his fatherhood to his biological descendants, however much he loved them.

He was also a father to many others, often more by

who he was than by anything particular he did. Certainly he played a fatherly role toward many of us here at St. Paul's. Certainly that is what he did as a mentor with Bridge Builders Counseling. And as St. Joseph helped Jesus recognize his Father in heaven, so I think our Joe helped many of us recognize that same Father in heaven. He was for many of us, like his New Testament namesake, a shadow of the Father, a gentle reminder of the divine love which often works quietly yet always reliably.

On some church calendars, March 19 appears as the feast of St. Joseph. In the Episcopal Church we have a prayer for that day which begins by thanking God for raising up Joseph to be the guardian of Jesus and the spouse of Mary. The prayer then goes on to ask for divine help that we may imitate Joseph's uprightness of life and his obedience to God's commands.

What we're about today includes thanking God for raising up our Joe to be a guardian, a father, and a friend to so many of us. And perhaps the best way we can honor the memory of this man, this quiet yet influential man, is for us to pray that we may imitate, each in our own way, his uprightness of life and his devotion and obedience to God.

It's thus that this family resemblance between one Joseph and another—a resemblance of character—can continue on, through our lives and beyond, all to the glory of God and the good of the world that he made.

MAN OF WONDER, MAN OF BLESSING: HAROLD, AN ELDERLY MAN IN A BORDER TOWN

What heritage does the deceased leave to his or her survivors? Perhaps that person was, as a matter of character, open to the God of all the earth, and thus became a blessing to others. If so, then the completed life beckons the mourners to be themselves people of wonder, people of blessing.

As I look upon what I know of Harold, and what his family has shared with me, I see him as a man of wonder and a man of blessing.

He was a man of wonder in many ways. Not only did he read in front of the fireplace. Not only did he read his magazines *Michigan History and Michigan Natural Resources* and his books about the Civil War, but he spent much time outside in the open air, where he read and reflected on the tremendous book of nature and absorbed something of its Author's wisdom. He watched the seasons change here in Michigan for eight decades, and never wearied of the beauty and never grew too old to be a man of wonder. Harold lived in the same house for more than half a century, and having visited there, I can see why he never moved. He loved that vast expanse of blue water where Lake Huron meets the St. Clair River.

He loved the huge boats that travel that water in quiet majesty. He loved the Blue Water Bridge, that graceful arc uniting opposite shores, uniting neighbor nations. He saw the bridge from his window by day against the changing sky. He saw it by night, lighted against the darkness like a diamond necklace resting on black velvet. He loved that nation to the east—Canada—and went there often for dinner with Margaret, for football games in Sarnia, to visit relatives in Toronto.

Harold lived on Michigan's eastern edge, and every day he looked across the water at another country.

I wonder if sometimes this closeness to another country reminded him that here on earth we are never far from the next life, that we are never far from our heavenly country, and that there is no cause for fear, because our Father owns land on both sides of the river. I wonder if sometimes Harold looked out at the Blue Water Bridge sparkling in the blackness of a winter night, and was reminded that Christ is our bridge from here to a country better than any on earth, our heavenly country, our true and lasting home.

Perhaps he had such thoughts, for he was a man of wonder and saw something of how earth is charged with the grandeur of God.

Harold had a habit of rooting for the underdog, the little guy. He did this even when it meant deciding that his favorite football team had had enough wins for a while. He did this even when it meant speaking the unpopular truth.

"The Indians got pushed out of their homes," is what Harold would say. He loved Indian people and their artifacts. Certainly their reverence for all the earth helped reinforce his own sense of wonder at the world around him. I feel Harold would agree with this observation made by

St. Gregory of Nyssa, "Concepts create idols; only wonder comprehends anything."

Only wonder comprehends anything! It's not that concepts or facts or knowledge are unimportant; they are very important. But it is only through wonder that they come to life, that they sparkle and shine and enrich our existence.

It is this wonder that we find in scientist and scholar, in mystic and poet, if they are at all worthy of their name, and it is this wonder that we find as well in a man who lived some fifty years on Michigan's eastern edge beside the Blue Water Bridge.

Harold was a man of wonder. And from that wonder came blessing. He was a man of blessing in ways that, perhaps, we do not understand, in ways that, perhaps, we will not understand on this side of our heavenly country.

His life was a blessing for many of us. That shone through in his love for his family, especially Margaret, his devoted wife; Sandra and Don, daughter and son-in-law; their daughters and sons-in-law and grandchildren. Harold blessed his family through his love and his example, and he blessed his friends as well. His wonder bore fruit in blessings for many, and continues to bear fruit, and for that we offer thanks today.

Some verses from Psalm 16 stand out for me as though Harold spoke them. I am so bold as to offer these verses as a kind of epitaph for him:

My boundaries enclose a pleasant land;
indeed, I have a goodly heritage.

I will bless the Lord who gives me counsel;
my heart teaches me, night after night.

I have set the Lord always before me;
because he is at my right hand I shall not fall.

My heart, therefore, is glad, and my spirit rejoices;
my body also shall rest in hope.

For you will not abandon me to the grave,
nor let your holy one see the Pit.

You will show me the path of life;
in your presence there is fullness of joy,
and in your right hand are pleasures for evermore.
(Psalm 16:6–11, *The Book of Common Prayer*)

And where is he now? We pray that he takes his place in that countless throng clothed in white, who hold in their hands palm branches—emblems of victory—and celebrate the victory of God and the Lamb.

In words we hear from the Revelation to John:

They are before the throne of God,
and worship him day and night within his temple,
and the one who is seated on the throne will shelter
them. They will hunger no more, and thirst no
more;
the sun will not strike them,
nor any scorching heat;
for the Lamb at the center of the throne will be
their shepherd,

and he will guide them to springs of the water
of life,
and God will wipe away every tear from their eyes.
(Revelation 7:15–17)

But what about us who are not there yet? Our task is
to share with one another what Harold meant to us and
continues to mean. Children and grandchildren, family
members and friends, we are to maintain the heritage he
left us. We can do this best once we understand that we,
like Harold, are to be people of wonder, people of blessing.

SOUL CLAP ITS HANDS AND SING: JOE, AN OLD MAN WITH A YOUNG HEART

*The key to preaching at a funeral may be something
from literature or art that was important to the
deceased. It may be a biblical story that the person
lived in a unique way. This sermon marshals
Shakespeare and Yeats as well as scripture to present
a portrait of a good and delightful old man whose wit
bore witness to God.*

It was only a few days ago that I stood beside Joe's hospital bed and watched him sleep. He opened his eyes. He
recognized me. And this is what he said, "All the world's
a stage, And all the men and women merely players; They
have their exits and their entrances, And one man in his
time plays many parts, His acts being seven ages. . . . Last
scene of all, That ends this strange eventful history, Is

second childishness, and mere oblivion, Sans teeth, sans eyes, sans taste, sans everything."[1]

He said these lines from Shakespeare without hesitation, and with a twinkle in his eye.

Well, Joe, now it is my turn. I owe you one! It seems to me that these Shakespearean lines, for all their elegance, tell but half the story.

For the other half, let me turn to an Irish poet, William Butler Yeats. He was a public figure down in Dublin when you were a child in Belfast. Here are some lines he wrote late in life:

> An aged man is but a paltry thing,
> A tattered coat upon a stick, unless
> Soul clap its hands and sing, and louder sing
> For every tatter in its mortal dress.[2]

Despite what Shakespeare wrote, the last scene of all is not oblivion, sans everything. The last scene is not, in fact, the last scene. Something more awaits us, if only our hearts are ready. And so, "Soul clap its hands and sing, and louder sing for every tatter in its mortal dress."

Let me tell you the story of how one soul came to clap its hands and sing.

Yesterday, on the Sunday between Joe's death and the day of his burial, the Church celebrated a feast called the Presentation of Our Lord Jesus Christ in the Temple. It comes every year forty days after Christmas. For it is forty days after his birth that Mary and Joseph bring Jesus to the Temple. There they make the offering that Jewish law requires in the case of a firstborn son.

While there in the Temple with their baby, the young couple encounter a man named Simeon. He is an old man, righteous and devout. Moreover, it has been revealed to him by the Holy Spirit that he will not die until he sees the long-awaited messiah.

It is the Holy Spirit that moves Simeon to visit the Temple on this day. When the parents bring in Jesus, Simeon takes the child up in his arms and sings a song of praise to God. Perhaps you know the words:

> Lord, you now have set your servant free
> to go in peace as you have promised;
> For these eyes of mine have seen the Savior,
> whom you have prepared for all the world to see:
> A Light to enlighten the nations,
> and the glory of your people Israel.
>> (Luke 2:29–32, *The Book of Common Prayer*
>> translation)

What Simeon sings leaves Mary and Joseph speechless, for he identifies their little baby as the promised messiah. The old man then blesses the young couple. He speaks also of the future, and how Mary will see her son put to death. "This child is destined for the falling and the rising of many in Israel," he says, "and to be a sign that will be opposed so that the inner thoughts of many will be revealed—and a sword will pierce your own soul too." (Luke 2:34b–35)

With these words, the aged Simeon steps off the stage of the biblical story and into the eternity of God.

The Church has never forgotten the song that Simeon sang. It has become a treasured part of worship, and is sung to countless settings and in many languages. Usually it appears in evening services, once daylight has disappeared, night has come, and we are reminded of our mortality.

Simeon and his song teach us about how to live and how to die. Simeon teaches us that what awaits us is not mere oblivion, sans everything, a final scene that brings all to an end. Instead, though an aged man is but a paltry thing, a tattered coat upon a stick, still soul clap its hands and sing, and louder sing for every tatter in its mortal dress, for these eyes of mine have seen the child of promise cradled in his mother's arms, and so, Lord, you have set your servant free.

I see Joe as another Simeon, the Simeon of St. Paul's. For he was here among us as a righteous and devout man, always looking for the Lord and so always finding him.

He was the oldest member of this parish, but I think he had the youngest heart. He saw the face of Christ in every child; he gave inspiration to every adult; and his presence here among us was a blessing. His graciousness, grown strong under the burden of life's losses, made real for us the poet's words: "Soul clap its hands and sing, and louder sing for every tatter in its mortal dress."

Now he has left us to be clothed with that immortal life which awaits the faithful in the world to come. I am sure that he will wear it well, and that he will clap his hands and sing, and louder sing for the healing which is his in that place, and the reunion with loved ones he never forgot, and for the glorious vision of the eternal Trinity. Yes, his soul will sing, and louder sing.

Because in this life he saw salvation even as old Simeon did. The Christ was there with Joe in his good hard work on the shop floor, and in the years of his marriage to his beloved Ann, when he felt on top of the world. The Christ was there as he sat and looked out on the wild and ever-changing surface of Lake Huron, never resting, ever moving.

The Christ was there too when he quoted lines of Shakespeare on his hospital bed, and did it with a twinkle in his eye, as if to say to me: This is splendid stuff, but only half the story. "Take it from me," he seemed to say, "An aged man is but a paltry thing," but "soul clap its hands and sing, and louder sing for every tatter in its mortal dress."

Yes, Joe, your life here was a song, and we thank you for the grace with which you sang it. The grace was God's gift. So too is the glory that awaits you. Now you can go in peace. And your song will never end.

---

1 William Shakespeare, *As You Like It,* Act II, Scene vii.
2 "Sailing to Byzantium," in Oscar Williams, ed., *A Pocket Book of Modern Verse*, rev. ed. (Washington Square Press, 1958), p. 187.

A Pointer to Ongoing Worlds

A GREAT GRIEF, A GREAT HOPE:
IAN, WHO LIVED LESS THAN A DAY

One of the hardest pastoral tasks is to preach at a baby's funeral. Here the homilist truly walks on holy ground through frightful country. It is tempting to say nothing in an effort to avoid irreverent, meaningless chatter. But this is a time when gospel hope must be proclaimed simply, clearly, quietly. The mourners, especially the parents, need a verbal portrait of the child that transcends the little casket in front of them. The agony of earthly loss cannot be denied, but a picture can be presented of that child among the blest in heaven, safe forever. The key is a heaven that offers hope on earth.

What brings us together today is a great grief and a great hope.

Our great grief is the loss of Ian. It was only hours after his birth that he died. For family and friends, the joy of this child's arrival was soon overshadowed by the pain of his departure. The long waiting through months of pregnancy came to an utterly unexpected conclusion.

To Lisa and Stewart, this loss is a horrible shock, but in their suffering they are not alone. Each of us—whether relative, neighbor, friend, parishioner—feels this pain in our own way. We are drawn together by grief. The loss of Ian is our loss, too.

An event as tragic as this exercises an irresistible influence on each one of us. We cannot remain where we are. We are forced to go in one direction or the other. One direction leads us to see this life as all there is and all there ever will be. In this direction, death appears as nothing more than darkness, and the universe is devoid of ultimate significance. The other direction leads us to see this life as offering the promise of a greater one. In this direction, death means change, not climax, and a providence does direct the universe, even though it exceeds our ability to imagine.

Which direction will we take? We cannot remain where we are. This tragic event forces us to go one way or the other. Either we submit to the cold embrace of despair, which offers no compassion and no hope, or we fall into the loving arms of God, a Father who knows what it's like to lose a child, for his Son died on the cross.

What brings us together today is a great grief and a great hope.

Our great hope is based on the resurrection of Jesus. Death was not the climax for him. He rose again in glory. Now he is our source and center for a life that cannot be destroyed. Our hope lets us see Ian even now as one of that great crowd which rejoices forever around the throne of God. How his soul must ring out with joy, that soul which never sinned, whose song is so innocent and pure! God's child through Baptism, protected by his presence, Ian is forever safe, and I have no doubt that in the communion of saints he prays for us all.

This hope, based on Jesus' resurrection, is meant not

only for Ian, but also for us. Resurrection hope tells us that Ian's death is not the end for him, and resurrection hope tells us that Ian's death is not the end for us, that just as there is new life for him, so there is new life for us.

With our grief and our hope come new life, renewed understanding, a fresh sense of what we know already, but need to learn again.

The loss of our small brother Ian reminds us that Jesus was once a baby, that as a man he wept for the dead, that his body was once cold and dead. Our human experience is not alien to him. He remains in solidarity with us.

The loss of our small brother Ian reminds us how fragile human life is—not only the life of a newborn child, but the life of everyone on earth. There are no strangers here. We are responsible for each other.

The loss of our small brother Ian reminds us that God does not ask us to be successful, intelligent, or attractive. God asks us for something more important: that we show compassion to all who share this life with us.

Other than hold him in our prayers, we can do nothing more for Ian. But remembering him can do a great deal for us. It can remove the hardness from our adult hearts. It can make us more compassionate toward those around us.

It can resurrect us once again to live a life of love.

DEATH NEVER HAS THE LAST WORD: EDDIE, A YOUNG MAN KILLED IN AN AUTO ACCIDENT

A young man dies in a car crash, leaving behind a son and daughter who will soon be teenagers. The good news of Jesus means eternal life for the deceased and a way out of the valley of death's shadow for those who mourn him. The keys to this sermon are the children themselves, their father's living legacy, who embody how God's love is stronger than death.

This gathering of Eddie's family and friends includes residents of the Port Huron area together with loved ones from Virginia. Eddie's brother Eric is here from Virginia Beach with his wife, Christine, and their children, Lindsay, Matthew, and Marissa. Please know, those of you who have come so far, that you are welcome in this church and this community.

There will be a time later in this service for any who wish to do so to share memories and thoughts of Eddie, and I hope that many of us will stand up and speak. Each of these recollections is a treasure, and a treasure we do well to share.

Months have passed since Eddie's funeral in Florida, yet no doubt a question still echoes in the heart of each of us who loved him. That question is: Why? Why did this happen to a gracious, energetic man who had so much to live for, whose life was starting to come together in new ways? Why did this happen as it did to Angela and Eddie, to Nancy, to all of us? Why?

It is natural and normal to ask this question. That we do so testifies to the weight of our loss. It demonstrates how we wanted, how we expected Eddie to continue as our companion on life's journey for many, many years to come.

A death like this slaps us in the face, and we want an explanation. We want to know who's responsible, who's to blame, who's the bad person in the picture. We want rationality, cause and effect, a fair universe, even if we must bear the guilt ourselves. We want to figure out this loss, make sense of it, get under control what feels to us so painfully out of control. No doubt each of us here has felt this struggle inside us sometime along this road of grief, and there may be people here who feel this terrible struggle right now.

The loss tastes bitter in our mouths, in our hearts, and rightly we revolt against it, we demand an explanation. Maybe we are told that what afflicts us, this grief that has attached to it a beloved name and face, is part of the human condition, evidence of a flawed universe, a world radically incomplete. But in this we find precious little comfort. We find little comfort there, and we are right. We have missed nothing, for there is little comfort to be found.

The good news of Jesus Christ looks at death, looks squarely at it, and refrains from offering an explanation, or assigning responsibility, or making sense of a loss too deep for words. What happens is something better, far better. The good news of Jesus Christ, once dead on the cross, and now—this moment—alive with glory, this good news offers us the strength, the hope, the grace to live through what is before us, to walk, bloody but un-bowed, through the valley of the shadow of death, in the firm and certain hope that God has prepared for us beyond that valley a much better mountaintop, a welcome table with all who love him, where God wipes away the tears from every face, and the people will say, "The Lord has saved us! Let's celebrate. We waited and hoped—now our God is here" (Isaiah 25:9 CEV). Yes, this good news of Jesus! We hear it and believe it, and it is good news now.

Picture this. It's nighttime, and we're gathered with many others in some great public building. The lights go out. Every last one of them. Lights outside and inside. We're in this great public building with all these people, and suddenly it's as though we're deep underground in a cavern, a place so dark you can't see the hand in front of your face. In that circumstance, I will wonder for a moment why the lights went out, the reason for it, but my real concern will be, who's got the flashlight?

When somebody dies, especially a young adult with every reason to live, then I will ask, why? I will ask it more than once. But more than an answer, I need a guide, a companion, somebody with a flashlight. I want somebody who can take me to the other side of grief. Somebody who promises me the opposite shore of death because he's been there and come back.

The Gospel announces a Father who's no stand-off-somewhere spectator to death, someone aloof and un-concerned. When it comes to the death of another thirty-something man, a man named Jesus, God the Father sits in the first row of mourners.

The Gospel announces a Savior who makes new life available free to us because it comes at such a cost to him. This Son of God tastes death, drains it to the dregs, for the sake of us and all people.

The Gospel announces a God who knows what death is about, who knows the weight of grief, a God who suffers with us, a God who suffers for us. So the Gospel does not bring an explanation of death, an apportionment of responsibility, but a surprise announcement of resurrection, the unexpected gift of hope. Our God never lets death have the last word—not for Jesus, not for Eddie, not for any of us who believe.

What I want to say now is intended for Angela and Eddie, though everyone else is welcome to listen.

Angela and Eddie, I speak to you not simply as your pastor, this guy who dresses up funny on Sundays, or as an adult, a person with some gray hair and lots of years on him. I speak as someone who feels a special connection with you because, like you, I also lost a parent to death when I was growing up. My mother died of cancer when I was seven. This was, as you can imagine, the defining event of my childhood.

Back then, people generally were less accepting of grief than we are today. Often a child's grief went largely unrecognized. People simply didn't know what to do with it. We live in a time now that seems to me more emotionally honest. I hope you feel free to express your grief to those who love you. I hope you are able to ask for what you need from us. There are resources to help you that did not exist when I was a child. Nobody can take away your grief, but perhaps we can help you make it easier to bear as you make your way to a new place of contentment.

Remember always that your father was a good man, and that he loved you, indeed, that he loves you still. I'm sure that, like every parent, he struggled with the best way to express his love. We parents do not come equipped with all the answers. We learn as we go along how to be a father, how to be a mother. Remember the special times with your father, especially the golden days of last summer, and recall them often in your heart as you might look at a special photograph.

Know that now your father is closer to God than he ever was before. He prays for you in a greater way than he ever could on earth. Pray for him yourselves, Angela and Eddie, pray for him during the years to come that he may continue to grow in God's love.

Certainly there were things your father wanted to do on earth that he was not given the time to do. Yet he leaves a tremendous legacy. You, Angela and Eddie, are that legacy, a living legacy. There's something of your father in each of you—in your appearance, in how you act, in what you say. Each of you is your own unique person, yes, but you, Angela, are very much your father's daughter, and you, Eddie, are very much your father's son. That resemblance, that heritage, is a blessing.

Your father had dreams and hopes for you. Like any loving parent, he wanted his children's lives to be even better, happier, and more complete than his own. I'm sure he also had dreams and hopes for himself, and looked forward to a long life.

Angela and Eddie, by the way you live your lives, by living with honor, compassion, and joy, you can realize the dreams your father had for you, and even the dreams he had for himself. You are his legacy, and a wonderful legacy you are. Live your lives well.

A SUCCESSION OF WORLDS:
MARGARET, RESIDENT IN THREE COUNTRIES

Some people in the course of life live in a succession of worlds, each one a markedly different place or period. Faith reminds us that the same God is present with them in each of those worlds, and that in Christ death is yet another transition, the final journey home.

I want to extend a heartfelt welcome to all of you who have come this day to celebrate Margaret's life, to recall all that she has meant to us and all that she continues to mean. Especially I want to welcome those of you from Canada who are here today.

It is appropriate that this be such an international gathering. For Nanna, in the course of her long life, lived in a succession of worlds. Born in Ireland, she went from there to England before traveling to this continent. She spent many years in Windsor before she relocated to Sarnia, and made many trips across the border here to Port Huron.

Nanna lived in a succession of worlds. The first was Ireland in the early years of this century. I imagine that among those of us here today there are few, perhaps none, who remember Nanna's childhood, or know firsthand the world where it took place.

Let me describe that world by borrowing some words from Herbert O'Driscoll, a priest of the Anglican Church of Canada who, like Nanna, started out in County Cork early in this century. He writes:

> In Ireland the ghosts of kings speak in place names. As you drive southwest from Cork City, you are driving toward a kingdom, the Kingdom of Kerry. The way to this kingdom is through a land that becomes increasingly lonely and rugged as you travel. The coastline, whenever you come to it, at places such as Ballingeary, is rugged and deeply indented from its struggle with a fierce and cold Atlantic. Now and again there are beaches that call the traveler by their beauty, as the sirens once called Ulysses and his crew. Like the sirens, they promise more than they provide. To walk these beaches is to taste the luxury of silence and solitude; to swim from them is to freeze the bones of even the bravest. Like any kingdom worthy of the name, these borderlands between Cork and Kerry have about them a touch of magic.[1]

Nanna lived in a succession of worlds. We have heard memories recalled of the several worlds where she lived in Canada and the United States.[2] I am sure that inside many of us there remain still other memories of this dear woman stored away like the best china and the family silver. Let me encourage you to share even more of these good memories in the months and the years ahead. Let Nanna's delightful laugh echo again through what we remember.

Yes, Nanna lived in a succession of worlds. Now she has been called forth to yet another one, one beyond our sight, but a world of unending beauty, the best world, the truest one she has ever seen. In each of these worlds where she once lived there waited for her the one God, the true God, the living God, who was the same in Ireland and England, in Ontario and Michigan.

The face of Christ was there for her to see in the faces of her family and her friends and the people who passed her in the busy street, whether that street was in London or Sarnia or Port Huron. The same Christ met her when she went to worship, whether it was in some ancient parish church in the British Isles, or St. Barnabas in Windsor, or here in this place. And that Christ was there for her as well in the natural beauty that delighted her in each of her successive worlds.

When she was a schoolgirl so long ago, perhaps she learned this poem written by an Irishman who died in 1916:

> I see his blood upon the rose
> And in the stars the glory of his eyes,
> His body gleams amid eternal snows,
> His tears fall from the skies.

I see his face in every flower;
The thunder and the singing of the birds
Are but his voice—and carven by his power
Rocks are his written words.

All pathways by his feet are worn,
His strong heart stirs the ever-beating sea,
His crown of thorns is twined with every thorn,
His cross is every tree.[3]

Yes, wherever Nanna went through the succession of her worlds, the one God, the true God, the living God was there to meet her. And now she has made the final transition, her entrance into that shining city which needs no light of lamp or sun, for God and the Lamb are its unending light.

Since I became a father for the first time late last year, there are many things I have noticed about the behavior and experience of babies. Something that happens to babies on a daily basis is that they fall asleep in one place and wake up to find themselves in another place. While the baby sleeps, someone carefully carries it to another location.

This is what happens to each of us early in life. We fall asleep in one place, and we wake up in another. This also happens at the end of life. We fall asleep in one place; we wake up in another.

Nanna lived in a succession of worlds. She fell asleep for the final time. She awoke. She awoke to find that the

One who had carried her from each world to the next through a succession of worlds had finally brought her home.

---

1 Herbert O'Driscoll, *The Leap of the Deer: Memories of a Celtic Childhood* (Cowley Publications: Cambridge, MA, 1994), p. vii.

2 This sermon was immediately preceded in the service by a time of sharing memories of Nanna, some of them riotously funny.

3 "Christ in Creation" by Joseph Mary Plunkett.